POSTER COLLECTION

CONTEMPORARY IRAN

35

Herausgegeben von / Edited by Bettina Richter

Essay von / by Majid Abbasi

T0349665

MUSEUM FÜR GESTALTUNG ZÜRICH
PLAKATSAMMLUNG / POSTER COLLECTION

LARS MÜLLER PUBLISHERS

1 **Morteza Momayez**
Doorguzabad
1976

VORWORT

Das iranische Plakat erregte erstmals um 2000 globale Aufmerksamkeit. Sozio-
politische Reformen und eine kulturelle Öffnung des Landes förderten damals den
internationalen Austausch auf der grafischen Bühne. Neben Morteza Momayez
(1935–2005), einem Pionier des modernen iranischen Grafikdesigns, schenkten auch
jüngere Gestalterinnen und Gestalter ihre Arbeiten der Plakatsammlung des Museum
für Gestaltung Zürich. 2021 trug der Grafiker Majid Abbasi rund 200 weitere zeitgenössische Plakate zusammen. Damit verfügt die Plakatsammlung heute über einen
reichen Bestand, der ein umfassendes Bild der grafischen Kultur des Iran erlaubt und
ihre Entwicklung in den letzten 50 Jahren reflektiert.

Momayez war dank seiner Ausbildung in Teheran und Paris ein idealer Mittler zwischen den Welten. Gemeinsam mit einigen anderen förderte er in den 1960er-Jahren
insbesondere das Medium Plakat und etablierte 1969 Grafikdesign als Disziplin an
der Fakultät der Bildenden Künste der Universität Teheran. Die Ausrufung der Islamischen Republik 1979 bedeutete jedoch einen radikalen Bruch, der Erste Golfkrieg
schnitt den Iran in den 1980er-Jahren zusätzlich vom Rest der Welt ab. Der bereits
vorher einseitige Blick des Auslands blendete nun kulturelle Ereignisse fast voll-
ständig aus. Gestalterinnen und Gestalter, die in diesen Jahren der internationalen
Isolierung ihre Ausbildung absolvierten, orientierten sich weiterhin an den Werken
der Pionierphase und beeinflussten wiederum die Nachkriegsgeneration.

Trotz vielseitiger Zugriffe prägt die Suche nach einer Verbindung von Historie und
Zeitgenossenschaft, eigenen Wurzeln und westlicher Inspiration, Kunst und Alltags-
kultur bis heute das iranische Plakatschaffen. Die fortwährende Auseinandersetzung
mit der persischen Schriftkultur und ihre Übersetzung in die Gegenwart stehen exem-
plarisch dafür. Im typografischen Bewusstsein der Moderne sind nicht-lateinische
Alphabete nur marginal vertreten und werden kaum als universale Schriftsysteme
rezipiert. Hinzu kommt, dass die komplexe Farsi-Schrift erst spät digitalisiert wurde.
Das westliche Auge nimmt sie meist verklärend als rein ornamentale, spirituell auf-
geladene, ästhetische Formen wahr, die zunehmende Abstraktion der Zeichen wird
wenig gewürdigt. Verstärkt wird dieser eurozentrische Blick durch eine oft symbo-
lisch verschlüsselte, poetische Bildsprache, die auch deshalb entwickelt wurde, um
Einschränkungen des Regimes visuell zu durchbrechen.

Der anhaltende internationale Erfolg des iranischen Plakats verdankt sich seiner
nationalen Originalität inmitten globalisierter Tendenzen. Für zeitgenössische Gestalterinnen und Gestalter bedeutet dies aber auch einen stetigen Balanceakt: die eigene
Kulturtradition annehmen, sie innovativ und zeitgemäss interpretieren – und sich
gleichzeitig sowohl jeder politischen Vereinnahmung durch das Regime als auch den
westlichen Verklärungen einer vermeintlich «orientalischen Ästhetik» widersetzen.

Bettina Richter

FOREWORD

The Iranian poster first attracted global attention around the year 2000, a time of sociopolitical reforms and cultural opening in the country that made room for international exchange in the graphic arts. During this period, Morteza Momayez (1935–2005), a pioneer of modern Iranian graphic design, along with some younger designers, donated works to the Poster Collection of the Museum für Gestaltung Zürich. Graphic artist Majid Abbasi then contributed a group of around two hundred additional contemporary posters in 2021. As a result, the Poster Collection now boasts a rich inventory that allows for a comprehensive survey of the evolution of Iran's graphic design culture over the past fifty years.

Educated in both Tehran and Paris, Momayez served as an ideal mediator between the two worlds. In the 1960s, he worked alongside several others to promote the poster medium in particular and established graphic design as a discipline in the Faculty of Fine Arts at the University of Tehran in 1969. The proclamation of the Islamic Republic in 1979 then marked a radical caesura, with the Iran-Iraq War in the 1980s cutting Iran off even further from the rest of the world. The already limited view of the country now almost completely ignored cultural events taking place there. Graphic designers who completed their training during these years of international isolation drew inspiration from the pioneering phase of Iranian graphic art, and their work would in turn influence the postwar generation.

Despite the versatile approaches displayed by today's Iranian posters, they are united by a search for reconciliation between historical and contemporary trends, between the designers' own roots and Western inspiration, between art and everyday culture. Exemplary for this quest is a pervasive engagement with the Persian written culture and its translation into the present. In modern typography, non-Latin alphabets play only a marginal role and are rarely acknowledged as the universal systems of writing that they are. Furthermore, it took a long time for the complex Farsi script to be digitized. The Western eye usually sees such non-Latin writing as purely ornamental, as spiritually charged aesthetic forms, and few are able to appreciate the evolving abstraction of the characters. This Eurocentric view is only reinforced by a visual language that is often symbolically encoded and poetic – a language that was developed in no small part as a way to circumvent restrictions imposed by the regime.

The enduring international popularity of the Iranian poster owes much to its originality as a national phenomenon amidst a plethora of global trends. For contemporary designers, however, this singularity also entails a constant balancing act: accepting their own cultural traditions and interpreting them in an innovative and contemporary manner while at the same time resisting political appropriation by the regime as well as a Western gaze that attributes to them a supposedly "Oriental aesthetic."

Bettina Richter

2 **Mohammadreza Abdolali**
Sky & Earth / Sculpture Collection Ghodratollah Agheli
2011

3 **Ghobad Shiva**
Festival of Arts Shiraz / Persepolis
1969

4 **Saeid Forootan**
Theatrical Kiss / A Film by Karim Lakzadeh
2018

5 **Studio Kargah / Sanaz Soltani**
Arya Tabandehpoor / Corruption, Retooling, Connection
2018

6 **Reza Abedini**
20ᵉ Festival international de l'affiche et
du graphisme de Chaumont
2009

TAMGA

Выставка 100 Иранских Логотипов

Кураторы Ибрагим Хагиги, Маджид Аббаси & Ариа Касаи

Международная биеннале товарных знаков и логотипов ТаMga`10

Россия, Новосибирск, Улица Ермака, 4

25 Ноября – 20 Декабря, 2010 . Открытие выставки, 25 Ноября (18:00)

www.tamga.biz

7 **Majid Abbasi**
100 Iranian Logotypes / Exhibition
2010

GRAFIKDESIGN IM IRAN IM SPIEGEL DER GESCHICHTE

Majid Abbasi

Die Originalität des iranischen Grafikdesigns beruht darauf, dass es einerseits die Grundlagen zeitgenössischer Gestaltungsansätze übernimmt und andererseits die Stilmittel und Formensprache der jahrhundertealten Kultur bewahrt, in der es wurzelt. In anderen muslimischen Ländern hat sich keine vergleichbare künstlerische Praxis herausgebildet. Insofern ist das iranische Grafikdesign einzigartig.

– Alain Le Quernec[1]

Ein flüchtiger Blick auf einige tausend Jahre iranischer Geschichte und visueller Kultur lässt zwei Epochen erkennen: die vorislamische Periode, die von den antiken Künsten der Bildhauerei, des Reliefs, der Architektur und der Keramik geprägt ist, und die islamische Zeit, die sich durch ihre Schrift und Kalligrafie auszeichnet. Diese heiligen Künste kommen in Manuskripten, Steininschriften, in der Architektur und später auch in der Herstellung und Gestaltung von Büchern zum Ausdruck, von Ornamenten und Malereien begleitet. Wenn es um die neuere Geschichte des Grafikdesigns geht, sind die letzten 150 Jahre relevant. Dieser Zeitraum lässt sich politisch in die Kadscharen-Dynastie (1789–1925), die Pahlavi-Dynastie (1925–1979) und die Islamische Republik (1979–heute) unterteilen. Zwei Ereignisse, die die Geschichte des Irans epochal veränderten, fallen in diese Zeit: die Konstitutionelle Revolution (1905–1911) und die Islamische Revolution (1979).

Während der Kadscharen-Herrschaft gewann der schiitische Islam an Macht, und im Zuge dessen zeigten sich Innovationen in Kunst und Literatur, beispielsweise in der Kalligrafie, Musik, Architektur, Poesie und Prosa. Die diplomatischen Beziehungen zu Russland und Grossbritannien wurden ausgebaut, und aus dem Westen importierte man wegweisende Technologien, so auch die Druckkunst. Die Einführung der Lithografie war eine Reaktion auf eines der wichtigsten Bedürfnisse der sich entwickelnden Gesellschaft. Dank der progressiven Entscheidungen von Abbas Mirza, dem reformorientierten Kronprinzen, konnte in den 1820er-Jahren in Täbris die erste Druckerei gegründet werden, und bewegliche Druck- und Lithografiemaschinen hielten Einzug im Iran.[2] Theaterplakate und staatliche Ankündigungen waren die ersten bekannten grafischen Arbeiten aus dieser Zeit. Erstere waren kleinformatig und auf farbigem Papier gedruckt, enthielten Illuminationen und Illustrationen, kombiniert mit handgeschriebenen und gedruckten persischen oder römischen Buchstaben. Um die Jahrhundertwende und im Zuge der Weiterentwicklung der Drucktechnik gewannen satirische Zeichnungen für Bücher und Zeitschriften sowie Illustrationen an Beliebtheit. Sie dienten dazu, soziale und politische Ungerechtigkeit, die Scheinheiligkeit der Geistlichen, die westliche Kolonialisierung sowie die Korruption der oberen Klassen anzuprangern, während gleichzeitig die Ideen der Bildungsreform und der Frauenrechte unterstützt wurden.

1 Alain Le Quernec, «Un cri persan», in: Radio Zones (Hg.), *Un cri persan,* Ausst.-Kat. Salon du livre de Genève, Genf 2008, o. S.
2 Abbas Amanat, *Iran. A Modern History,* New Haven / London 2017, S. 252.

Während der Konstitutionellen Revolution entwickelte sich die Presse, und die Verbreitung von Informationen in Form von Bekanntmachungen, Büchern, Zeitungen und Zeitschriften nahm zu. Nach dem Staatsstreich 1921 errichtete Reza Khan die Pahlavi-Dynastie, reformierte Bildungs- und Justizeinrichtungen und legte den Grundstein für einen modernen Staat, indem er den Einfluss der religiösen Schichten schmälerte. Während des Zweiten Weltkriegs und nach der Besetzung des Irans durch die Alliierten dankte Reza Shah zugunsten seines Sohnes Mohammad Reza[3] ab. Die Regentschaft des neuen Königs war geprägt von einem relativ offenen gesellschaftspolitischen Umfeld, das zur Veröffentlichung von Büchern, Zeitschriften und zur Entwicklung gesellschaftspolitischer und kultureller Kompetenzen beitrug. Gegen Ende der 1940er-Jahre gewann, im Gleichschritt mit der Popularität des Filmemachens, das Grafikdesign für das Kino an Bedeutung und wurde allmählich zu einer ernst zu nehmenden, eigenständigen Disziplin. Zu deren Vorreitern gehörten Mohammad Bahrami, Sadegh Barirani 70, Mahmoud Javadipour und Houshang Kazemi. Inspiriert von ihrem kulturellen Erbe entwarfen sie Plakate, Buchumschläge und Logos für staatliche und private Institutionen.

In den 1950er- und 1960er-Jahren entstanden in Japan und in osteuropäischen Ländern wie Polen bedeutende länderspezifische Trends, die weltweit Einfluss nahmen und sich auch auf das iranische Grafikdesign auswirkten. Unter Premierminister Mohammad Mossaddegh wurde die Ölindustrie verstaatlicht. Im Jahr 1953 putschte der Schah, stürzte Mossaddegh und festigte seine Macht. Mit dem Anstieg der Ölpreise in den frühen 1970er-Jahren florierte die Wirtschaft und begünstigte die politischen Ambitionen des Schahs, dessen Regime zunehmend autoritär wurde.[4] Parallel zu den sozioökonomischen Veränderungen im Iran traten die einflussreichen Grafikdesigner Farshid Mesghali, Morteza Momayez und Ghobad Shiva in Erscheinung. Obwohl sie alle einen Abschluss in Malerei hatten, beriefen sie sich – von den damaligen Entwicklungen in der Illustration und im Grafikdesign beeinflusst – auf die Wurzeln der visuellen Kultur Persiens, der nationalen Malerei und Kalligrafie, um ihre eigenen Werke in Form von Plakaten, Buch- und Zeitschriftenumschlägen, Illustrationen für Magazine sowie Logos und Schriftzüge zu schaffen. In den 1960er- und 1970er-Jahren unterstützte die Regierung nationale und internationale Kunstveranstaltungen. So erhielten Plakatgestalterinnen und -gestalter Aufträge von zahlreichen Organisationen und Festivals, Kinos und Theatern. Ihre Plakate wurden zu einer Fundgrube für herausragendes Grafikdesign und inspirierten die nächste Generation. Gruppen- und Einzelausstellungen in der Ghandriz Hall und anderen Galerien, insbesondere *50 Years of Iranian Graphic Design* (1976) und die First Asian Graphic Design Biennial in Teheran (1979), gehörten zu den wichtigen Veranstaltungen, die vor der Islamischen Revolution 1979 stattfanden.

Die Plakate von Morteza Momayez – 1977 erstes iranisches Mitglied der Alliance Graphique Internationale (AGI) – für das Internationale Filmfestival in Teheran sowie

3 Ebd., S. 415–416.
4 Ebd., S. 551.

für unabhängige Filmregisseure sind hervorragende Beispiele für iranische Plakate aus dieser Zeit. Seine kontrastreichen Bilder und Collagen, die teilweise von polnischen Grafikdesignerinnen und -designern inspiriert sind, setzten im Zusammenspiel mit seiner einzigartigen Typografie die zahlreichen, für verschiedene Zeitschriften- und Buchumschläge geschaffenen Illustrationen fort 1, 56–58, 61–62, 124. Ghobad Shiva bewies seine einzigartige Begabung in der Illustration und der handgezeichneten Typografie in den für das Kunstfestival in Schiras 3, 22 und für das staatliche iranische Radio und Fernsehen gestalteten Plakaten. Wie Momayez und Farshid Mesghali schuf auch Shiva Illustrationen für verschiedene Zeitschriften, von denen einige von der Arbeit der Push Pin Studios in New York beeinflusst sind. Mesghali, Träger des Hans Christian Andersen Award (1974), zeigte seinen originellen kindlichen visuellen Ausdruck und seine Handschrift auf den Plakaten des Institute for the Intellectual Development of Children and Young Adults 73, 75.

Die Entwicklung an den Universitäten und Schulen spielte in den vergangenen siebzig Jahren eine entscheidende Rolle bei der Ausbildung von Grafikdesignerinnen und -designern. Als Hauptfach wurde die Disziplin zum ersten Mal in den 1960er-Jahren an der Hochschule für Kunstgewerbe in Teheran unter Houshang Kazemi unterrichtet, der selbst Grafikdesign in Paris studiert hatte. Mitglieder der Fakultät waren Franzosen oder Iraner, von denen aber einige ebenfalls in Europa studiert hatten.[5] Damit bot sich den Studierenden die Möglichkeit, sowohl von der Erfahrung und den Kenntnissen der visuellen Tradition Persiens als auch von den Grundsätzen der westlichen Kunst und des westlichen Designs zu profitieren. Darüber hinaus wurde in den 1970er-Jahren an der Fakultät der Bildenden Künste der Teheraner Universität ein Grafikdesignkurs in den Lehrplan des Fachbereichs Bildende Kunst aufgenommen. Dank der Anstrengungen von Momayez und seiner Kollegen, die von der École nationale supérieure des arts décoratifs in Paris inspiriert waren, wurde Grafikdesign in den 1980er-Jahren als eigenständiger Studiengang anerkannt, der Kurse wie die Grundlagen der visuellen Kommunikation, Illustration, Kalligrafie und Schriftgestaltung, Geschichte der islamischen Kunst, Geschichte der Presse und des Buchwesens, Fotografie und Handdruck umfasste.[6] Momayez, die Bildhauer Karl Schlamminger und Parviz Tanavoli sowie der Kalligraf Mohammad Ehsaei gehörten zu den Lehrern, die die Studierenden ermutigten, sich auf ihr kulturelles Erbe zu besinnen und es mit den internationalen Grundlagen der visuellen Kommunikation zu kombinieren. Später trug die Entstehung von Bildungszentren wie der islamischen Azad-Universität (1980er-Jahre) und der Vije School of Visual Communications (2004) zur qualitativen und quantitativen Ausbildung im Grafikdesign bei, die in den letzten zwei Jahrzehnten durch Privatkurse ergänzt wurde.

1979 errichtete Ayatollah Khomeini die Islamische Republik. Ein Jahr später marschierte der Irak in den Iran ein, und das Grafikdesign stand im Dienst des Krieges und der Werte der Revolution. Mohammad Chatamis Präsidentschaft (1997–2005)

---

5 Kamran Afshar Mohajer, «Art and Crafts», in: *Neshan*, Nr. 5 (Winter 2005), S. 17.
6 Alireza Mostafazadeh, «Starting Point», in: *Neshan*, Nr. 5 (Winter 2005), S. 14.

ging einher mit Forderungen nach gesellschaftspolitischen Reformen und einem offeneren Klima. Das Verlagswesen und das Grafikdesign für Zeitungen, Zeitschriften und Bücher entwickelten sich weiter. Eine neue, von der New-Wave-Typografie des Westens angeregte Generation von Gestalterinnen und Gestaltern erlangte internationale Anerkennung für ihre Betonung der Ästhetik der persischen Kalligrafie und für ihre typografischen Fähigkeiten, die das Grafikdesign in qualitativer und quantitativer Hinsicht vorantrieben 6, 27–35, 46–47, 71, 114. So erschienen beispielsweise Schrift und Typografie in verschiedenen Formen neben dem Bild: Sie interagierten mit dem Bild, vermischten sich mit ihm oder bildeten sogar das Bild selbst. Diese Plakate zeichnen sich durch eine spielerische Anordnung der Buchstaben, eine experimentelle Typografie, Anspielungen auf die klassischen Regeln der Kalligrafie und deren Dekonstruktion sowie durch die Verwendung von Handschrift aus 2, 7–8, 13, 19, 26. Gedruckt wurden sie hauptsächlich im Offsetdruck, oftmals aber auch im Siebdruck oder digital, Auftraggeber waren typischerweise Kulturbetriebe. Diese Plakate waren nur an Orten mit begrenzter Reichweite im Aushang, beispielsweise in Galerien, Kinos, Theatern, hausinternen Aushängen oder in den Schaufenstern von Cafés oder Buchläden, jedoch nicht auf den Strassen.

In den zwei Jahrzehnten nach der Islamischen Revolution fanden sieben Grafikdesign-Biennalen statt (1987–2001), auf denen Verpackungen, Buch- und Zeitschriften-umschläge, Plakate, Typografie und Logogestaltung präsentiert wurden. Diese Biennalen wurden von Momayez und seinen Kollegen gemeinsam geleitet und unter der Schirmherrschaft des Ministeriums für Kultur und islamische Führung, des Teheraner Museums für zeitgenössische Kunst und der 1997 gegründeten Iranian Graphic Designers Society (IGDS) organisiert. Aufgrund der offeneren gesellschaftspolitischen Situation ab 1997 wurden zum ersten Mal seit der Islamischen Revolution auch eine Reihe von internationalen Grafikdesignerinnen und -designern eingeladen, ihre Werke auf der 6. und 7. Biennale 1999 und 2002 auszustellen. Der Austausch der iranischen Grafikdesign-Szene mit der Aussenwelt wurde 2002 auch durch die Ausstellung *Un cri persan* von Alain Le Quernec im Rahmen des Mois du graphisme d'Échirolles gefördert, einem Designfestival in der Nähe von Grenoble. Entscheidend dafür, dass das iranische Grafikdesign weltweit bekannt wurde, war das Magazin für Grafikdesign *Neshan* (2003–2020), das von einer Gruppe von Grafikdesignern gegründet und auf Farsi und Englisch veröffentlicht wurde. Obwohl eine begrenzte Anzahl von Printexemplaren auch nach Übersee geschickt wurde, blieb die Online-Version die einzige und auch effektivste Quelle für iranisches Grafikdesign.[7] Das Magazin wurde 2020 wegen finanzieller Probleme und inhaltlicher Unstimmigkeiten zwischen den Herausgebern eingestellt.

Die IGDS spielte zusammen mit anderen Verbänden und Nichtregierungsorganisationen eine wichtige Rolle bei der Durchführung der Biennale. Nach der siebten Ausgabe wurde sie in Tehran International Poster Biennial umbenannt und noch

---

7 Majid Abbasi, «About *Neshan*», www.neshanmagazine.com/About.aspx?l=2.

zweimal, in den Jahren 2004 und 2007, von der IGDS organisiert. Dann intervenierte die Regierung, die Plakat-Biennale wurde eingestellt; seit 2010 werden die Arbeiten der IGDS-Mitglieder unabhängig und ohne staatliche Unterstützung im Rahmen des Silver Cypress Award ausgestellt. Dieser Preis umfasst Grafikdesign für Buch- und Zeitschriftencover, Visual Identity, Verpackungen, Schriftgestaltung und digitale Arbeiten und lädt internationale Grafikdesignerinnen und -designer ein, mit ihren Werken teilzunehmen. Zudem gründete die IGDS im Jahr 2015 das Iranian Museum of Graphic Design, das den Weg für eine Fachausbildung bereiten und eine fundierte Quelle für die Studierenden sein soll. Sein Ziel ist es, das öffentliche Bewusstsein für Grafikdesign zu schärfen und über die Archive des Museums nationale und interna- tionale Beziehungen zu fördern.[8]

Mit dem Beginn der Präsidentschaft von Mahmud Ahmadinedschad im Jahr 2005 begann eine neue Ära der Hardliner-Regierung, die darauf abzielte, die früheren Frei- heiten wieder einzuschränken. Das Militär baute seinen Einfluss aus und dominierte die meisten Staatsämter. 2013 gewann zwar der gemässigte Geistliche Hassan Rohani die Wahlen, dieser wurde 2021 aber vom ultrakonservativen Ebrahim Raisi abgelöst, seither werden die Restriktionen wieder härter. Die erneute Verhängung internationaler Sanktionen aufgrund des Rückzugs der USA aus dem Joint Compre- hensive Plan of Action (Atomabkommen) 2018, der Ausbruch der Covid-19-Krise sowie andere interne Konflikte setzten dem internationalen Austausch ein Ende. Der gewaltsame Tod von Jina Mahsa Amini löste 2022, vor dem Hintergrund grundlegen- der Freiheitseinschränkungen und der Wirtschaftskrise, eine massive Protestbe- wegung aus, die insbesondere von Frauen und Jugendlichen angeführt wird und die Regierung vor die grösste Herausforderung seit der Islamischen Revolution von 1979 stellt. Zum ersten Mal werden gesellschaftspolitische visuelle Botschaften entworfen und in grossem Umfang über soziale Medien verbreitet, um mit der Aussenwelt zu kommunizieren.

Die iranische Plakatgestaltung lässt sich besser verstehen, wenn man mit der tradi- tionellen iranischen Kunst und Kultur und deren Einfluss auf das moderne Grafik- design vertraut ist. Legten frühere Grafikdesigner den Schwerpunkt auf die Illustra- tion, so betonen zeitgenössische Designerinnen und Designer die Typografie. In den vergangenen zwei Jahrzehnten zeichnete sich das iranische Plakatdesign dadurch aus, dass es das Potenzial von Schrift und Typografie nutzte, was zur Entstehung einer nationalen visuellen Sprache führte, die von einer Reihe historischer epochaler Veränderungen im weltweiten Grafikdesign beeinflusst wurde, insbesondere durch neue digitale Technologien. Die zeitgenössischen Plakate haben die Grenzen der ira- nischen Plakatgestaltung erweitert und zeigen die Energie, Leidenschaft und Begeis- terung einer Generation moderner Gestalterinnen und Gestalter, die in einem alten Land einen einzigartigen Stil entwickelt haben.

8 «About the Museum» (in persisch), Iranian Museum of Graphic Design, 2022, www.igds.ir/moze.

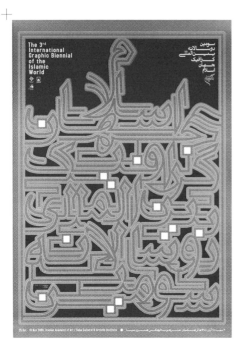

8 **Amir Hossein Ghoochibeik**
The 3rd International Graphic Biennial of
the Islamic World, 2009

9 **Masoud Nejabati**
The Celebration of Eid al-Ghadir
2019

10 **Masoud Nejabati**
The Celebration of the Birth of Imam Reza
2012

11 **Majid Abbasi**
International Conference on Masterpieces
of the Persian Painting, 2005

12 **Masoud Nejabati**
The Celebration of the Birth of Imam Reza
2011

13 **Mojtaba Adibi**
Almajoghi Ali Bakhshi / Dutar Playing for Quchan
2013

14 **Studio Fa / Mahdi Fatehi**
The 7th Iranian Folk Music Festival
2011

15 **Masoud Nejabati**
Exhibition of Fine Arts / Professors and Students
2001

16 **Studio Kargah / Peyman Pourhosein**
The Wedding by Tarlan Rafiee
2010

17 **Mehdi Saeedi**
The 17th Fadjr International Music Festival
2002

18 **Mehran Zamani**
The 1st Fadjr Handicrafts & Traditional Arts Festival
2017

19 **Mehdi Saeedi**
14th Fortnight Festival Music Zekro-Zakarin
2004

20 **Farzad Adibi**
Roar of Silent / Khorosh-e-Khamosh
2007

21 **Reza Babajani**
2nd Esfand Drawing Annual
2017

22 **Ghobad Shiva**
5th Festival of Arts Shiraz / Persepolis
1971

23 **Iman Safaei**
27 April / World Graphics Day
2008

My Soul is
Poured in You

Painting Group
Exhibition
Ida Rahimi/Iman Sadeghi
Ehsan Ahmadi/Anahita teimouri
Elham Abdolhoseinpour/AmirHossein Keihani
Javad Ghanbarpour/Hojat Nikravesh
Zahra Derogar/Shirin Babazadeh
Asal Hemmatian/Kasra Monemi
Nasim Etemadsarabi

13-17 Oct.2017
Opening:
Friday,13 Oct
Visiting Hrs:
5-10 p.m

Digari Art Gallery
No10.
22 southBozorgmehr.
Sajad Blvd.
Mashhad.
Iran
+9851 37600902
www.Digariartgallery.com
Info@Digariartgallery.com

24 **Reza Babajani**
My Soul Is Poured in You
2017

25 Mohammad Khodashenas
The Group Poster Exhibition in Studio Graphic Design
Mohammad Khodashenas
2009

26 Masoud Morgan
Knitted Camps / Setare Salehi Arashloo
2015

27 **Damoon Khanjanzadeh**
Kambiz Derambakhsh
2007

28 **Studio Kargah / Saam Keshmiri**
Nose to Nose
2018

29 **Reza Babajani**
Ismail Ghanbari / Abandoned
2016

30 **Majid Kashani**
Groupage / Photo Group Exhibition
2012

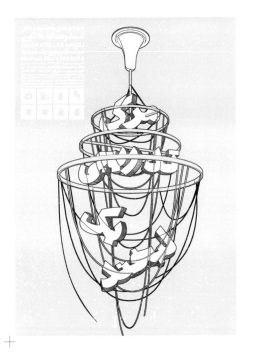

31 **ChapChin Studio / Davood Morgan, Javad Zarinia**
Solo Painting Exhibition / M. J. Pakravan / Siyavash in Fire, 2018

32 **Mohammadreza Abdolali**
Ghodratollah Agheli / Gradual Death of a Smile, 2013

33 **Damoon Khanjanzadeh**
Career Record / Unveiling Karnameh Publication Typeface, 2012

34 **Mohammadreza Abdolali**
Mohsen Mahmoodizade / Protect Me from What I Want, 2015

35 **Bijan Sayfouri**
Bouf-e Kour / Iranian Typography Exhibition
2003

36 **Bijan Sayfouri**
Khiyal / The Quarterly Periodical
of the Iranian Academy of the Arts
2002

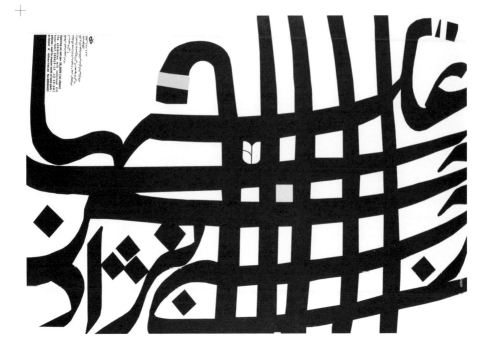

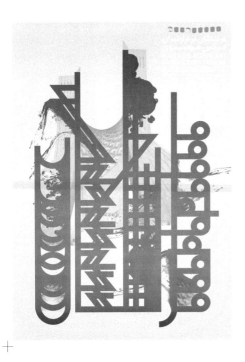

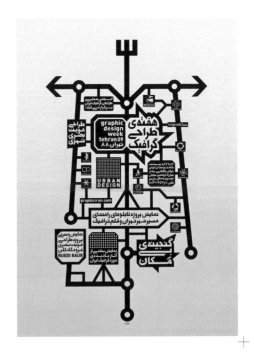

37 Mohammad Khodashenas
Hassan Rajabinejad / Photo Exhibition
2006

38 Studio Metaphor / Ali Asali
Narges Mousavi / Angels Over Tehran
2015

39 Studio Kargah / Aria Kasaei
Graphic Design Week Tehran 09
2009

40 Studio Metaphor / Ali Asali
Folding / Amir Farsijani
2016

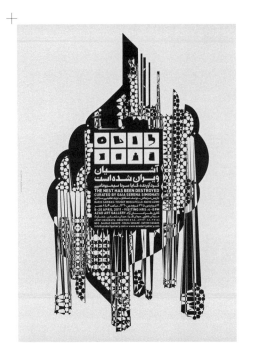

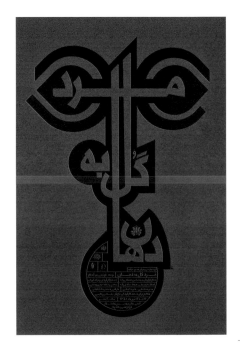

41 **Studio Kargah / Aria Kasaei**
The Nest Has Been Destroyed
2011

42 **Morteza Mahallati**
Rokhsat Poster Exhibition
2008

43 **Studio Fa / Mahdi Fatehi**
New York / Tehran / Group Street Art Exhibition
2014

44 **Reza Babajani**
A Man with the Flower in His Mouth
2009

45 **Studio Kargah / Aria Kasaei**
Bimzar
2010

46 **Reza Abedini**
Mehran Mohajer / Reza Abedini / Photo + Graphic
Exhibition, 2004

47 **Pedram Harby**
Tehran I Love You / Photography Group Exhibition
2013

48 **Bijan Sayfouri**
The 13th Tehran International Book Fair
2000

49 **Pedram Harby**
An Evening of Theater
1999

50 **Majid Abbasi**
A Mieczysław Wasilewski Retrospective in Tehran
2007

51 **ChapChin Studio / Davood Morgan,**
Javad Zarinia
Farzad Annual / Contemporary Drawing
2017

52 **Studio Metaphor / Ali Asali**
Tadaex / 6th Tehran Annual Digital Art Exhibition /
Tadagrant 2016
2016

53 **Studio Kargah / Peyman Pourhosein**
Plakart / On Iranian Cinema Marquee Posters
2017

54 **Studio Kargah / Peyman Pourhosein**
Cold Fire / An Overview of Photographs from the
Iran-Iraq War, 2018

55 **Studio Kargah / Aria Kasaei**
Chasm / Malek Foundation
2019

GRAPHIC DESIGN IN IRAN IN THE MIRROR OF HISTORY

Majid Abbasi

The notable originality of Iranian graphic design stems from its preservation of its deep-rooted culture even as it adopts modern ideas. This feature is unrivaled in the Islamic world, and it makes Iranian graphic design truly unique.

– Alain Le Quernec[1]

With a fleeting glimpse at some thousand years of Iran's history and visual culture, two epochs can be seen: the pre-Islamic period characterized by ancient arts of sculpture, relief, architecture, and pottery; and the period after the Islamization of Persia characterized by writing and calligraphy as ethereal arts in manuscripts, stone inscriptions, and architecture, and later the design and making of books accompanied by decorations and paintings. As far as the contemporary history of graphic design is concerned, the last 150 years are particularly relevant. This period could be politically divided into the Qajar Dynasty (1789–1925), the Pahlavi Dynasty (1925–79), and the Islamic Republic (1979–present). Also, in this period there were two epoch-making incidents that changed Iranian history: the Constitutional Revolution (1905–11) and the Islamic Revolution (1979).

During Qajar's rule, Shi'a Islam gained power and, parallel to it, innovations appeared in art and literature through calligraphy, music, architecture, poetry, and prose. Diplomatic ties with Russia and Britain were expanded and cutting-edge technologies from the West such as printing were imported. The importation of lithography was a response to one of the main needs of the developing society. As a result of the progressive decisions made by Abbas Mirza, the reformist crown prince, the first printing house was established in Tabriz (1820s) and movable type and lithography machinery made its way into Iran.[2] Theater posters and state announcements were the first known works of graphic design around this time. Theater posters were small in size, on colored paper, with illumination and illustrations, combined with handwritten and printed Persian and Roman letters. At the turn of the twentieth century, following the advancement in printing technologies, satirical drawings for books and magazines and illustrations gained in popularity. These illustrations were a tool to criticize social and political injustice, the hypocrisy of the clergy, Western colonization, and the upper class's venal corruption, while supporting the ideas of educational reform and women's rights.

During the Constitutional Revolution, the press was developed and the diffusion of information in the form of announcements, books, newspapers, and magazines increased. In 1921, Reza Khan staged a coup and established the Pahlavi Dynasty, reformed educational and judicial institutions, laid the foundations for a modern state, and reduced the influence of the religious classes. During World War II and

1 Alain Le Quernec, "Un cri persan," in *Un cri persan,* ed. Radio Zones, exh. cat. Salon du livre de Genève, Geneva 2008, n.p.
2 Abbas Amanat, *Iran: A Modern History,* New Haven / London 2017, p. 252.

after the Allies occupied Iran, Reza Shah abdicated in favor of his son Mohammad Reza.[3] A fairly open sociopolitical environment during the new king's reign led to the publication of books, magazines, and sociopolitical and cultural competence. Toward the late 1940s, with the popularity of filmmaking, graphic design for cinema gained ground and gradually became a serious field. Among the progenitors of this new field were Mohammad Bahrami, Sadegh Barirani 70, Mahmoud Javadipour, and Houshang Kazemi. Inspired by their cultural heritage, they designed posters, book covers, and logos for the state and for private institutions.

In the 1950s and 1960s, in Japan and in Eastern European countries such as Poland, decisive, nationally divergent trends in graphic design emerged that were of global appeal and that proved influential on Iranian graphic design. During the administration of Prime Minister Mohammad Mosaddegh, the oil industry was nationalized. The Shah staged a coup in 1953, overthrowing Mosaddegh and consolidating his power. With the increase in oil prices in the early 1970s, the economy flourished and fostered the Shah's political ambitions, his regime becoming increasingly authoritarian.[4] Concurrent with socioeconomic changes in Iran, influential designers Farshid Mesghali, Morteza Momayez, and Ghobad Shiva emerged. Although they were graduates of painting, influenced by contemporary changes in illustration and graphic design they tapped into the Persian roots of visual culture, national painting, and calligraphy to create their own works in the form of posters, book and magazine covers, illustrations for magazines, and logos and logotypes. In the 1960s and 1970s, the government supported national and international art events. Poster designers were commissioned by numerous organizations and festivals, cinemas and theaters. These posters ended up being a treasure trove of stellar graphic design and inspired the next generation. Group and individual exhibitions in Ghandriz Hall and other galleries, *50 Years of Iranian Graphic Design* (1976), and the First Asian Graphic Design Biennial in Tehran (1979) were among the important graphic design events held before the 1979 Islamic Revolution.

Posters by Morteza Momayez, the first Iranian AGI member (1977), for the Tehran International Film Festival as well as for independent film directors are excellent examples of Iranian posters from this era. His high-contrast images and collages, partly influenced by Polish designers, along with his unique typography are the continuation of his hundreds of illustrations for various magazines and book covers 1, 56–58, 61–62, 124. Ghobad Shiva used his unique skill in illustration and manual typography in designing posters for the Shiraz Festival of Arts 3, 22 and National Iranian Radio and Television. Like Momayez and Farshid Mesghali, Shiva also illustrated several magazines, some of which were influenced by the work of Push Pin Studios in New York. Mesghali, the recipient of the Hans Christian Andersen Award (1974), presented his original and childlike visual expression alongside handwriting for the posters of the Institute for the Intellectual Development of Children and Young Adults 73, 75.

3 Ibid., pp. 415–16.
4 Ibid., p. 551.

The development of universities and schools played a pivotal role in training graphic designers over the past seventy years. For the first time graphic design was taught as a major in the College of Decorative Arts, Tehran, in the 1960s under Houshang Kazemi, who himself had studied graphic design in Paris. Faculty members were French and Iranian, some of whom likewise had studied in Europe.[5] This combination provided an opportunity for the students to benefit from both the experience and knowledge of Persian visual roots as well as the principles of Western art and design. In addition, at the Faculty of Fine Arts, University of Tehran, a graphic design course was included in the curriculum of the Visual Arts Department in the 1970s. Through the endeavors of Momayez and his colleagues, who had been inspired by the École nationale supérieure des arts décoratifs in Paris, graphic design was recognized as an independent major in the 1980s, with the inclusion of such courses as Principles of Visual Communication, Illustration, Calligraphy and Type Design, History of Islamic Art, History of the Press and Bookmaking, Photography, and Manual Printing.[6] Momayez, the sculptors Karl Schlamminger and Parviz Tanavoli, and the calligrapher Mohammad Ehsaei were among the teachers who encouraged students to refer to their cultural heritage and combine it with international fundamentals of visual communication. Later on, the emergence of educational centers – Islamic Azad University (1980s) and Vije School of Visual Communications (2004) – contributed to the qualitative and quantitative teaching of graphic design, supplemented in the last two decades by private courses.

In 1979, the Islamic Republic was established by Ayatollah Khomeini. A year later, Iraq invaded Iran and graphic design was at the disposal of the war and revolutionary values. Mohammad Khatami's presidency (1997–2005) was concomitant with the need for sociopolitical reforms and a more open climate. The publishing industry and graphic design for newspapers, magazines, and books developed further. A new generation of designers, influenced by New Wave Typography in the West, established an international reputation for their emphasis on Persian calligraphy aesthetics and typographic capacities that impacted graphic design qualitatively and quantitatively 6, 27–35, 46–47, 71, 114. For example, type and typography appeared in various forms alongside the image: they interacted with the image, or mixed with it, or even formed the image itself. These posters are characterized by a playful composition of letters, experimental typography, an evoking of the classic rules of calligraphy combined with their destructuring, and the use of handwriting 2, 7–8, 13, 19, 26. They were typically commissioned by cultural institutions and primarily offset-printed, but often also screenprinted or printed through digital means. These posters were displayed in limited-reach venues such as galleries, cinemas, theaters, in-house bulletins, or on the windows of some cafés and bookstores, but not in the streets.

During the two decades after the Islamic Revolution, seven Biennials of Iranian Graphic Design were held (1987–2001) in order to showcase packaging, book and

5 Kamran Afshar Mohajer, "Art and Crafts," *Neshan* 5 (Winter 2005), p. 17.
6 Alireza Mostafazadeh, "Starting Point," *Neshan* 5 (Winter 2005), p. 14.

magazine cover design, posters, type design, and logo design. These biennials were organized by the collaborative direction of Momayez and colleagues under the aegis of the Ministry of Culture and Islamic Guidance, the Tehran Museum of Contemporary Art, and the Iranian Graphic Designers Society (IGDS), established in 1997. Due to the more open sociopolitical situation since 1997, for the first time after the 1979 Islamic Revolution a number of international graphic designers were invited to exhibit their works at the 6th and 7th Biennials (1999 and 2002), and Iranian graphic designers' interaction with the outside world was also fostered by Alain Le Quernec's exhibition *Un cri persan* at the Mois du graphisme d'Échirolles (2002), a design festival near Grenoble. *Neshan* graphic design magazine (2003–20), founded by a group of graphic designers and published in Farsi and English, played a significant role in the introduction of Iranian graphic design to the world. Although a limited number of printed issues were sent overseas, the online version remained the only, and most effective, resource on Iranian graphic design.[7] Its publication was discontinued in 2020 due to financial issues and member disagreement on the content.

IGDS along with other associations and NGOs played a determining role in holding the biennials. Having been held seven times, it was renamed the Tehran International Poster Biennial and organized again by IGDS twice, in 2004 and 2007. After government intervention, the Poster Biennial was discontinued and beginning in 2010 the IGDS members' work has been exhibited independently and without governmental support through the Silver Cypress Award. The award encompasses graphic design for book and magazine covers, visual identity, packaging, type design, and digital works, and invites international graphic designers to exhibit their creations. In addition, IGDS established the Iranian Museum of Graphic Design in 2015 to pave the way for specialized education, be a reliable source for scholars, elevate public awareness about graphic design, and expand national and international ties through the museum's archives.[8]

By the start of Mahmoud Ahmadinejad's presidency in 2005, a new era of hard-line governance had begun that aimed to limit the previous freedoms. Military forces expanded their clout and dominated most of the state offices. In 2013, the moderate cleric Hassan Rouhani won the elections, but since August 2021 the ultraconservative Ebrahim Raisi has been in power, and restrictions have since increased again. The reimposition of international sanctions due to the United States' withdrawal from the Joint Comprehensive Plan of Action (JCPOA) in 2018, the outbreak of Covid-19, and other internal conflicts put an end to the international exchanges. Against a backdrop of a fundamental lack of freedom and economic crises, the violent death of Jina Mahsa Amini sparked a massive protest movement in 2022 led specifically by women and youth; it has been the biggest challenge to the government since the 1979 Islamic Revolution. For the first time, sociopolitical visual messages are designed and distributed extensively through social media to communicate with the outside world.

7 Majid Abbasi, "About *Neshan*," *Neshan*, 2020, www.neshanmagazine.com/About.aspx?I=2.
8 "About the Museum" (in Persian), Iranian Museum of Graphic Design, 2022, www.igds.ir/moze.

An understanding of Iranian poster design becomes more complete accompanied by a familiarity with traditional Iranian art and culture and its influence on contemporary graphic design. As much as the early graphic designers emphasized illustration, contemporary designers accentuate typography. In the last two decades, Iranian poster design has been distinguished by capitalizing on the potential of type and typography, leading to the advent of a national visual language influenced by a number of historical epoch-making transformations in the world's graphic design, especially through new digital technologies. Contemporary posters have expanded the boundaries of Iranian poster design and showcased the energy, passion, and enthusiasm of a generation of contemporary designers who have developed an original approach in an ancient land.

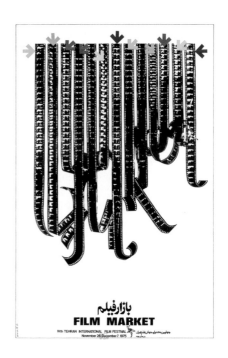

56 **Morteza Momayez**
Hommage an Pablo Neruda
1980

57 **Morteza Momayez**
Exhibition of Graphic Works / Morteza Momayez
ca. 1975

58 **Morteza Momayez**
Film Market / IVth Tehran International Film Festival
1975

59 **Ebrahim Haghighi**
Andrzej Wajda / Images of an Era
1989

60 **Shahab Tondar**
Painting Exhibition by Amirpasha Hoshivar
2010

61 **Morteza Momayez**
Hommage an Pablo Neruda
1980

62 **Morteza Momayez**
Buster Keaton: The Sentimental Face / IV Tehran
International Film Festival, 1976

63 **Mohammad Reza Dadgar**
Blind War
1979

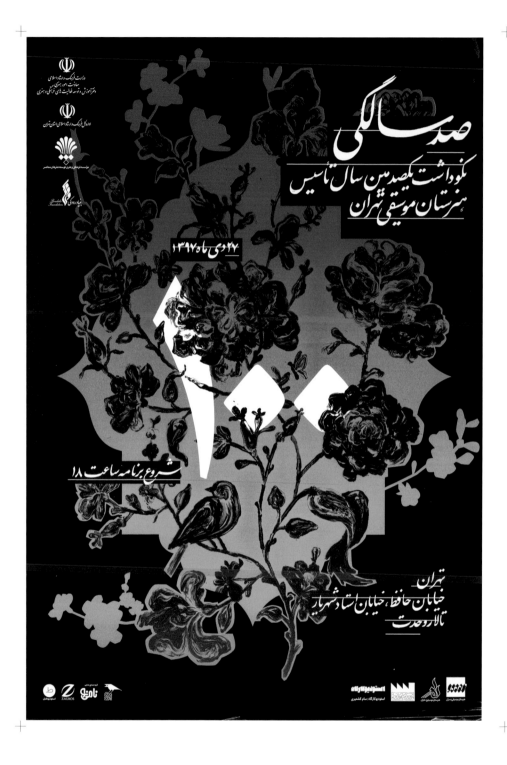

64　**Studio Kargah / Saam Keshmiri**
Celebrating the Centenary of Tehran Music Academy
2019

65 **Ghobad Shiva**
800th Anniversary of the Birth of Saadi,
Iranian Thinker, Poet and Writer
1984

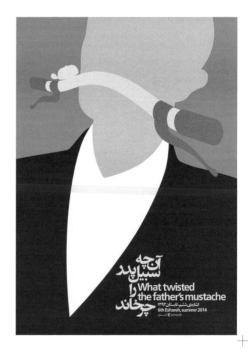

66 **Alireza Mostafazadeh Ebrahimi**
Nature Invites Us to Graphic Art. Graphic Art
Invites Us to Nature., 2003

67 **Alireza Mostafazadeh Ebrahimi**
Antigone
2009

68 **Alireza Mostafazadeh Ebrahimi**
Hello and Goodbye
2012

69 **Alireza Mostafazadeh Ebrahimi**
What Twisted the Father's Mustache
2014

70 **Sadegh Barirani**
Coppelia
1971

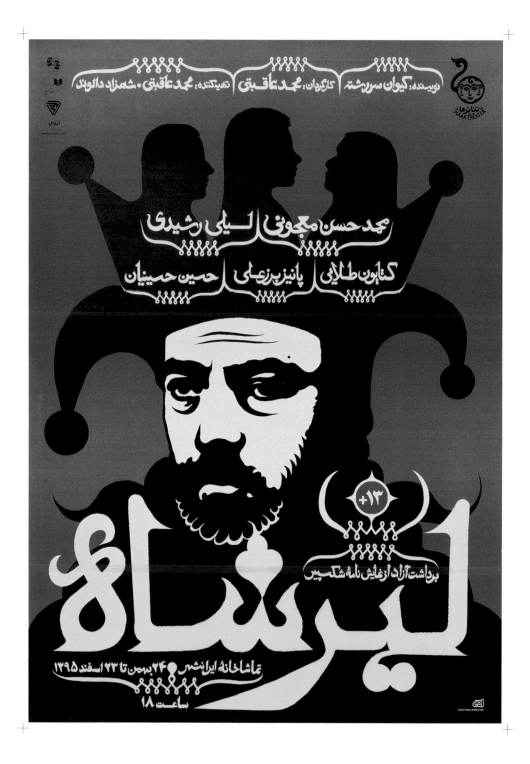

71 **Mojtaba Adibi**
King Lear
2017

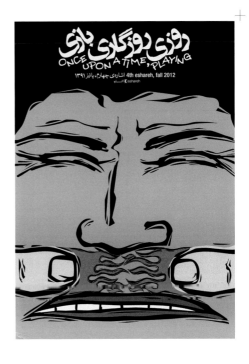

72 Siamak Pourjabbar
Anti-Gone
2018

73 Farshid Mesghali
Children Literature in the Service of International
Understanding and Peaceful Co-Operation, 1975

74 Alireza Mostafazadeh Ebrahimi
Once Upon a Time, Playing
2012

75 Farshid Mesghali
Polish Animation Films / 11th Tehran International Festival
of Films for Children and Young Adults, 1976

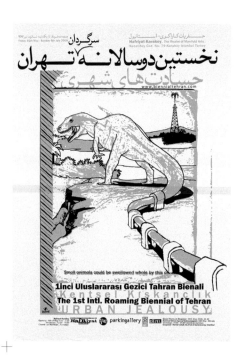

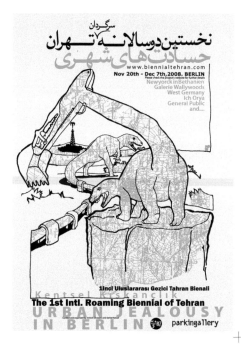

76 **Homa Delvaray**
Divarkoob / 49 Posters of 51 Graphic Designers
2010

77 **Amirali Ghasemi**
Urban Jealousy / The 1st Intl. Roaming Biennial of
Tehran / Kentsel Kıskançlık, 2008

78 **Siamak Pourjabbar**
Side by Side in Solidarity / Greeting from Iran
2011

79 **Amirali Ghasemi**
Urban Jealousy in Berlin / The 1st Intl. Roaming Biennial
of Tehran / Kentsel Kıskançlık, 2008

80 **Homa Delvaray**
Tehran Monoxide Project
2014

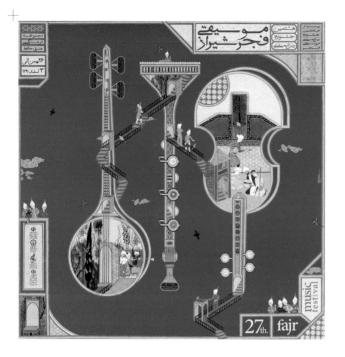

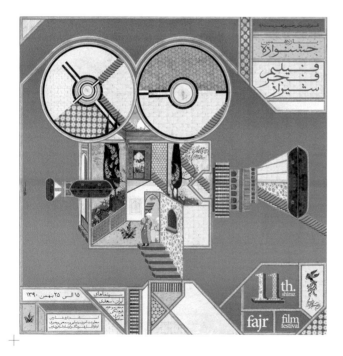

81 **Mehrzad Dirin**
27th Fajr Music Festival
2012

82 **Mehrzad Dirin**
11th Shiraz Fajr Film Festival
2012

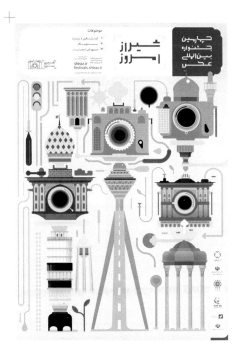

83 **Mehrzad Dirin**
4th Shiraz Today International Photo Festival
2017

84 **Majid Abbasi**
Streets of Tehran / A Selection of Mahmoud Pakzad's
Photographs, 2006

85 **Mohammad Khodashenas**
Samira Eskandarfar / There Is No Us
2019

86 **ChapChin Studio / Davood Morgan,
Farid Yahaghi**
World Urbanism Day, 2013

EIN SEMIPOETISCHER ÜBERBLICK ÜBER AKTUELLE IRANISCHE PLAKATKUNST ALS ZEITDOKUMENT

Maryam Razi

Die iranischen Plakate der vergangenen Jahrzehnte sind synästhetisch: Man *sieht* das Bild, aber *hört* die Stadt; man *liest* die Schrift, aber *fantasiert* von einer alten Geschichte; man *fühlt* die Farben, aber *riecht* die Gerüche der Strassen und Basare. Plakate sind eine Erweiterung der Lebensumgebung der Menschen, die sie gestalten, Menschen, die sich auch als Stadtbewohnerinnen und Stadtbewohner begreifen; implizit beschreiben sie den von Eindrücken erfüllten Weg von ihrem Zuhause in ihr Atelier. Iranische Plakate sprechen alle Sinne an, sind gleichzeitig Werbung und Dokumente ihrer Zeit. Ich denke dabei an Plakate, die sich rahmen lassen, die man studieren und archivieren kann, an die exzentrischen Arbeiten der Gestalterinnen und Gestalter, die die herkömmlichen Visualisierungscodes verändert und Plakate neu definiert haben, sodass sie mehr als nur Werbeobjekte sind.

Was heute als Bildkomposition bezeichnet wird, wurde nach alten persischen Schriftquellen *Skelett* genannt. Das symmetrische Skelett war die gängigste Anordnung der Elemente innerhalb eines Rahmens. Die choreografierte Augenbewegung begann in der Bildmitte und endete am Rand, multidimensional auf einer zweidimensionalen Leinwand wandernd. Diese voll entwickelte Struktur ist heute wieder populär, sie überflutet das Bildfeld spiegelbildlich mit Formelementen und erzeugt ein visuelles Déjà-vu. Iranische Plakate erzählen Geschichten, sie sind Raconteure. In einer Region, die so reich an Erzählungen ist, hat alles, was man auf eine Fläche zeichnet, sofort tausend mögliche Interpretationen.

Die Plakate sind Paradebeispiele für die visuellen Studien der Gestalterinnen und Gestalter. Sie verwenden eine Typografie, die persische Kalligrafiestile aktualisiert und weiterentwickelt, sodass sie zu ihrem zeitgenössischen Ansatz passt. Die Illustrationen auf den Plakaten sind reduzierte Versionen iranischer Miniaturen und Erzählungen, ihre Botschaften haben eine tausend Meilen lange Reise aus einer archaischen Geschichte hinter sich.

Die Haltung der Gestalterinnen und Gestalter und die Art und Weise, wie sie ihre Umgebung betrachten, haben das iranische Plakat aus dem Gleichgewicht gebracht. Sie repräsentieren die Essenz persischer Architektur und die Gelehrtheit der Künstlerinnen-Kunsthandwerker einer vergangenen Zeit, zugleich spiegeln sie das Lebensumfeld heutiger Gestalterinnen und Gestalter wider. Plakate sind so zu einem Medium für vielschichtige Erzählungen geworden. Das moderne Ethos der Stadt und ihre chaotische Erscheinung, die der reichen Architektur der Vergangenheit gegenüberstehen, sind auf den Plakaten in ständiger Bewegung: Die Zeit fliesst, persische Literatur und mythische Geschichten schimmern, das verführerische Wesen der Kalligrafie formt seine rhythmischen Bewegungen.

Iranische Plakate sind in Bezug auf Inhalt (Typografie und visuelle Elemente) und Kontext (Narration und Geschichte) im Wesentlichen retrospektiv – sie sind nicht Gegenwart, sondern stets «eine Sekunde davor».

Paradoxerweise blicken die jüngsten Plakate mit ihren zukunftsweisenden Ansätzen immer noch in die Vergangenheit, wie jemand, der rückwärtsgeht, um voranzukommen. Dieses herausragende Merkmal kennzeichnet ein Land, das reich an Bildern und Geschichten ist.

Der Charakter des persischen Alphabets ist fliessend. Es passt kaum in die definierten Rasterlinien, die Schrift streckt sich vielmehr frei über die Topografie. In den letzten zehn Jahren wird Schrift als eine Form der Bildgestaltung eingesetzt, meist ist sie dabei eher visuelle Erzählung als blosse Botschaft. Die gestalterischen Ideen manifestieren sich in der Typografie, das Rechteck des Plakats verwandelt sich in einen Spielplatz ohne Schwerkraft; Schrift spielt in diesem Drehbuch ihre wirkungsvolle Rolle.

Diese Plakate sind keine flüchtigen Werbeträger mehr, sondern archivierungs- und rahmungswürdige Dokumente einer lebendigen Generation, die die Vergangenheit schätzt und die Gegenwart festhält. Allmählich werden die Plakate unmittelbarer – es bleibt keine Zeit mehr für überbordende Poesie. Gerade Linien und verstreute Partikel ersetzen geschwungene und verschwommene Linien, alltägliche Geschichten bereiten die Reise. Ich nenne diesen Trend allgemein *Post-Reza-Abedini*[1] – wenn die Typografie auf einem Plakat nicht mehr poetische Erzählung, sondern anschauliches Motto ist.

Während ich diesen Text schreibe, befindet sich der Iran inmitten eines einzigartigen, von Frauen geführten Aufstands, der die Plakatgestaltung unweigerlich beeinflusst und beeinflussen wird. Die Botschaft, die die Plakate der vergangenen Monate übermitteln, springt den Betrachterinnen und Betrachtern ins Auge, ohne zu tanzen oder zu flirten, denn die Zeit ist knapp. Der Inhalt ist weniger vielschichtig, der Tanz der Typografie auf der Leinwand ist zu einem Marsch geworden. Das Plakat als Kommunikationsmedium wird an vorderster Front eingesetzt, es informiert und motiviert. Wir erleben einen visuellen Wandel: Die Plakate fangen den Zeitgeist der neuen Generationen in kräftigen Farben und lauten Tönen ein.

1 Reza Abedini (*1967) ist ein namhafter Grafikdesigner, der dafür bekannt ist, die persische Sprache in poetischen Typografiestilen zu erforschen.

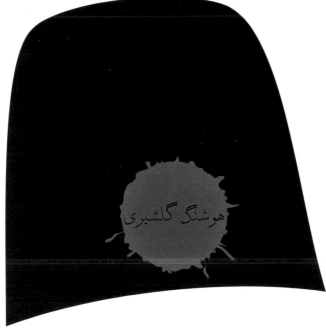

هوشنگ گلشیری

به یاد بود گلشیری، در سالمرگ نخستین

87 **Alireza Mostafazadeh Ebrahimi**
Houshang Golshiri / Prince Ehtejab /
First Memorial Service for Golshiri
2001

88 Mojtaba Adibi
Khat-e Khati / Abousaeed Eskandari
2019

89 Siamak Pourjabbar
Greed
2012

90 Mehran Zamani
The 14th Tehran International Ritual-Traditional Theatre
Festival, 2009

91 Studio Kargah / Saam Keshmiri
Homarg / Album by Baramant
2019

92 **Majid Kashani**
The Sound of One Hand
2013

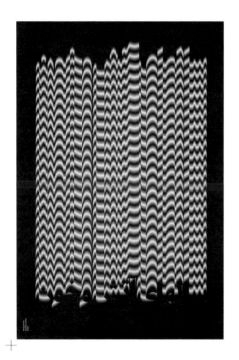

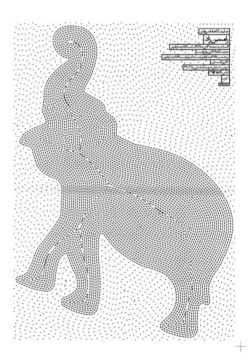

93 Studio Kargah / Sanaz Soltani
Land / Ali Phi
2017

94 Shahab Tondar
The Years of Fire and Blood
2020

95 Studio Kargah / Sanaz Soltani
Home / Gohar Dashti
2017

96 Iman Safaei
Ramtin Zad / Painting Exhibition
2007

97 **Studio Kargah / Peyman Pourhosein**
The International Congress of Shiraz School
2008

98 **Studio Kargah / Peyman Pourhosein**
Horses Stomp at the Window 1
2011

POSTER AS A FRAMEABLE DOCUMENT:
A SEMI-POETIC OVERVIEW OF THE CURRENT
POSTERS IN IRAN
Maryam Razi

The posters designed in recent decades in Iran are syn-esthetic: you *see* the image, but you *hear* the city; you *read* the type, and you *hallucinate* about an old story; you *feel* the colors, but in return you *smell* the scent of the streets and the bazaar. Posters are an extension of the designer's living environment, tacitly depicting the emotive path from the designer's home to the work studio. Traversing the senses, Iranian posters are simultaneously advertisements and documents of their time, and the designer is the citizen-designer. I am talking about such posters that are "frameable," "studiable," and "archivable." This text describes the eccentric works of designers who changed the standard visualization codes and redefined posters to be more than advertising objects.

Based on past Persian written resources, today's *composition* was called *skeletal*. The symmetrical skeleton was the most popular arrangement of the components within a frame. The choreographed eye movement would start with the central part and end at the margin, voyaging multidimensionally on a two-dimensional canvas. This fully developed structure is popular again in posters, overflowing the frame with visual elements in a mirror-like manner, generating a visual déjà vu. Iranian posters are storytellers and raconteurs. When *you* come from a region overwhelmed with tales, whatever you draw on a surface has thousands of interpretations.

Posters are the epitome of designers' visual studies. The typography placed on the poster is an updated version of Persian calligraphy styles, which the designer has refined to fit into a contemporary approach. The illustrations on the posters result from an abridged visual duplicate of the Iranian miniatures and narratives. Moreover, the message conveyed travels a thousand miles from an old archaic tale.

The designers' points of view on the subjects and how they observe their surroundings have made the posters of Iran off-kilter. On the one hand, posters represent the Persian architectural essence and the sagacity of the artist/artisan of the past. On the other, they reflect the contemporary life of the designer's living environment. Posters therefore have become a medium of multilayered narratives. The city's contemporary ethos and its chaotic mien opposing the rich architecture of the past are constantly in motion in the posters; time is fluid; Persian literature and mythical stories glimmer, and the alluring essence of the calligraphy creates a rhythmic movement within the frame.

Iranian posters are essentially retrospective in terms of content (typography and visual components) and context (narration and story) – not the present time but "just a second ago." Paradoxically, in the latest futuristic approaches taken by younger designers, posters are still looking back in time, like someone walking backward to move forward. This brilliant feature indicates a land rich in visuals and stories.

The personality of the Persian alphabet is fluid. It hardly fits in the defined grid lines, making the type extend freely across its topography. In the recent decade, the incorporation of type into posters is approached as a form of image-making, in most cases adding a visual narrative rather than a mere message. The designer's idea is incarnated in typography, and the rectangular shape of the poster turns into a non-gravitational playground; the type plays an effectual role in this screenplay.

No longer fleeting advertisement objects, posters are ultimately characterized as frameable archival documents of a living generation who appreciate the past and record the present. Posters are gradually becoming more straightforward – there is no more time to be overly poetic. Straight lines and scattered particles replace curved and blurry lines, and daily narratives build up the journey. I broadly call this trend the made-up name *post-Reza Abedini*,[1] in which typography on posters is no longer a poetic narration but a vivid motto.

As I write these words, Iran is in the midst of a one-of-a-kind female-led uprising, inevitably affecting the character of poster design. The message communicated through posters of recent months penetrates the viewer's sight without dancing or flirting, as time is short – the content is less layered, and the dance of typography on the canvas has transformed into marching. The poster as a communicating medium has been used on the front line, employing an informative and motivational approach. We are experiencing a visual shift in which the posters capture the zeitgeist of the new generations in bold colors and loud tones.

1 Reza Abedini (*1967) is a well-known graphic designer recognized for exploring the Persian language in poetic typographic styles.

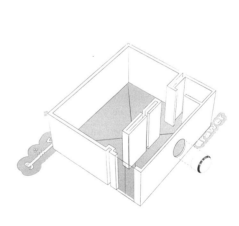

99 **Morteza Akoochekian**
Tehran; Lorzadeh / The Architect House-Museum
2019

100 **Morteza Akoochekian**
Settimana del cinema italiano
2018

101 **Morteza Akoochekian**
Khayyam / Millennium Anniversary
2018

102 **Amirali Ghasemi**
Drawer / Visual Snippets of "Chargoosh"
2007

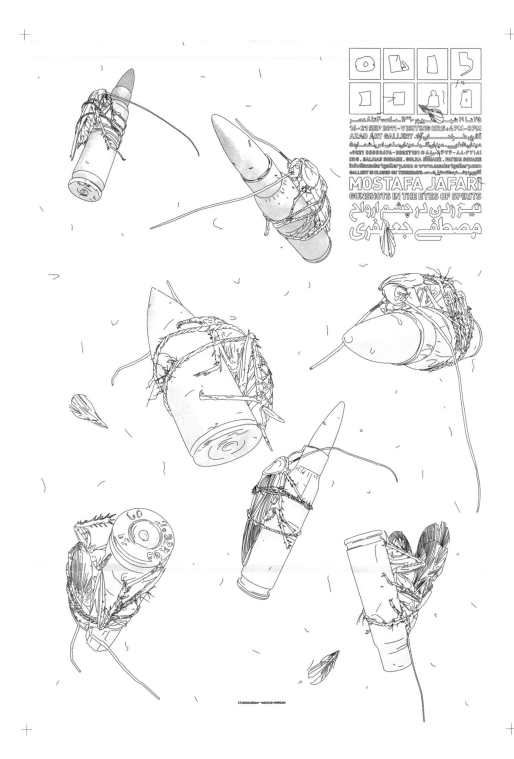

16-21 SEP 2011 · VISITING HRS: 4PM - 8PM
AZAD ART GALLERY

info@azadartgallery.com ★ www.azadartgallery.com
GALLERY IS CLOSED ON THURSDAYS

MOSTAFA JAFARI
GUNSHOTS IN THE EYES OF SPIRITS

103 **Studio Kargah / Masoud Morgan**
Mostafa Jafari / Gunshots in the Eyes of Spirits
2011

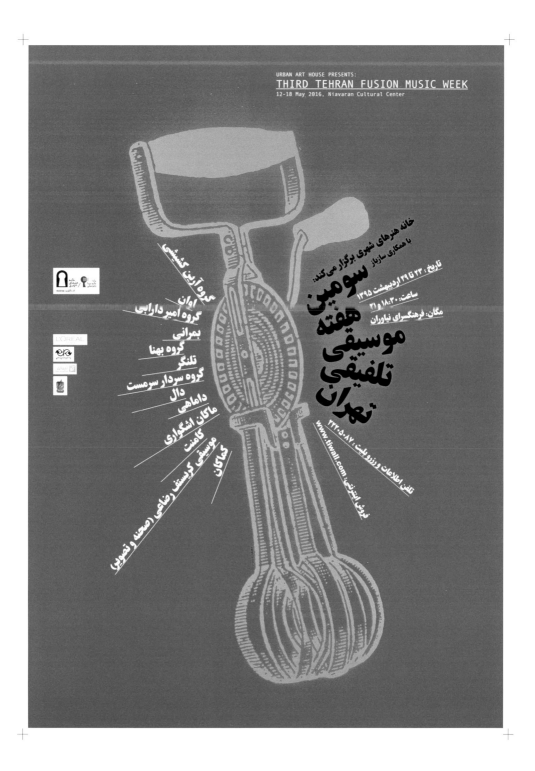

104 **Pedram Harby**
Third Tehran Fusion Music Week
2016

105 **Ebrahim Haghighi**
A Persian Requiem / Simin Daneshvar
2001

106 **Ebrahim Haghighi**
Me, Taraneh / 15 Years Old
2002

107 **Masoud Nejabati**
Exhibition of Fine Arts by Professors and Students
2002

108 **Saed Meshki**
The 3rd International Theatre Festival of Iranzamin
2001

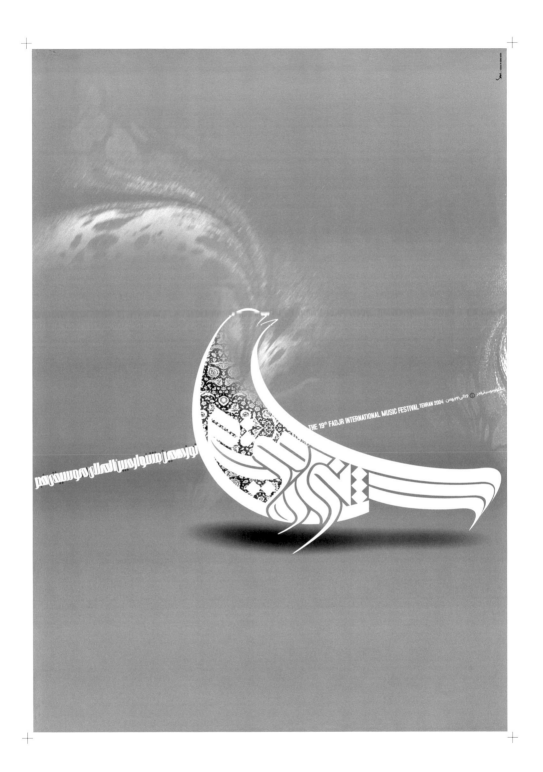

109 **Mehdi Saeedi**
The 19th Fadjr International Music Festival
2004

110 **Reza Abedini**
The 23rd Fadjr International Theater Festival / Tehran
2005

111 **Reza Abedini**
Painting Exhibition / Rezvan Sadeghzadeh
2005

112 **Reza Abedini**
AllOne / Reza Abedini
2006

113 **Studio Kargah / Sanaz Soltani**
Skin, Flesh, and Bone / Arya Tabandehpoor
2017

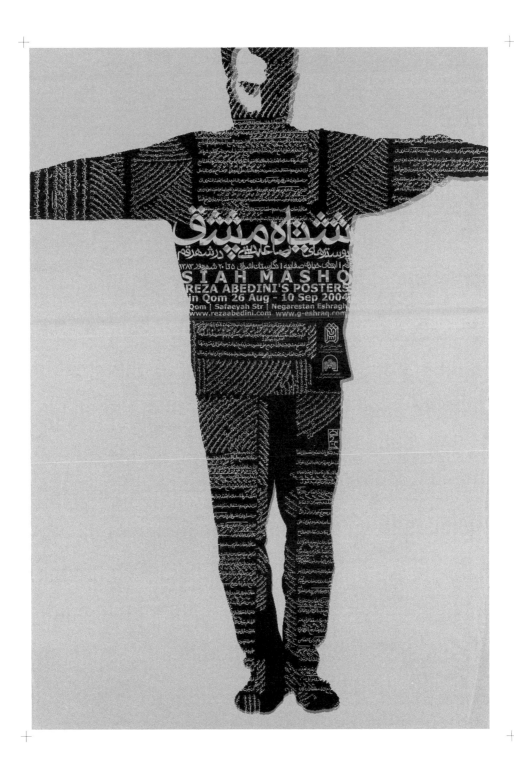

114 **Reza Abedini**
Siah Mashq / Reza Abedini's Posters
2004

115 **Saed Meshki**
Third Film Festival in Memory of the Abadan Uprising
2002

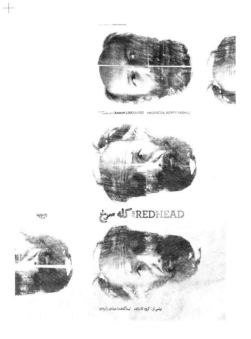

116 **Saeid Forootan**
The Redhead
2017

117 **Pedram Harby**
Final Encore II
2013

118 **Ali Khorshidpour**
Assemblage Art / Introducing French Contemporary
Artist Arman, 2003

119 **Pedram Harby**
Where Were You on January 8th?
2009

120 **Pedram Harby**
Ivanov
2011

121 **Majid Abbasi**
. . . in Memory of Kaveh Golestan
2003

122 **Majid Abbasi**
An Exhibition of the Photographs (Original Prints)
of Sadeq Hedayat, 2001

123 **Farzad Adibi**
Monthly Journal of Literature and Philosophy
2002

124 **Morteza Momayez**
The Custodian / A Film by Khosrow Haritash
1976

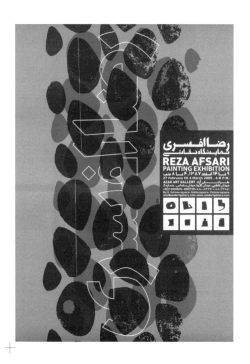

125 Reza Abedini
Reza Abedini / Complexion / Virtual Poster Exhibition!
2005

126 Reza Abedini
Reza Afsari / Painting Exhibition
2009

127 Reza Abedini
Raha Rastifard / I &...
2011

128 Reza Abedini
Parastou Forouhar / I Surrender
2009

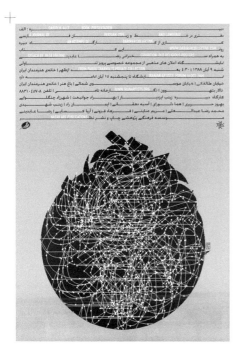

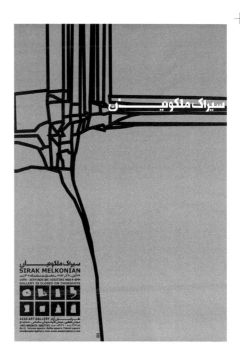

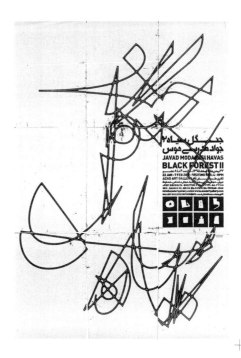

129 **Reza Abedini**
Book Presentation / Dabireh: Alef
2009

130 **Reza Abedini**
Hossein Maher / Painting Exhibition
2007

131 **Reza Abedini**
Sirak Melkonian
2008

132 **Reza Babajani**
Javad Modaresi Havas / Black Forest II
2017

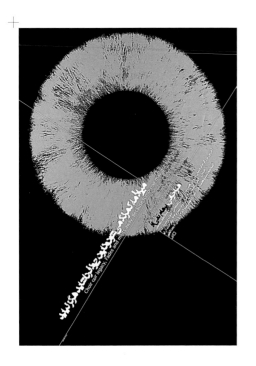

133 Pedram Harby
Choir: Our Legacy, Fades and Melts Away, Because
Tomorrow May Not Ever Be, 2003

134 Pedram Harby
Installation / Arash Yadollahi
2001

135 Pedram Harby
I'm Not a Story You Can Tell...
1999

136 Iman Safaei
Sculptures by Jolee / Julie
2007

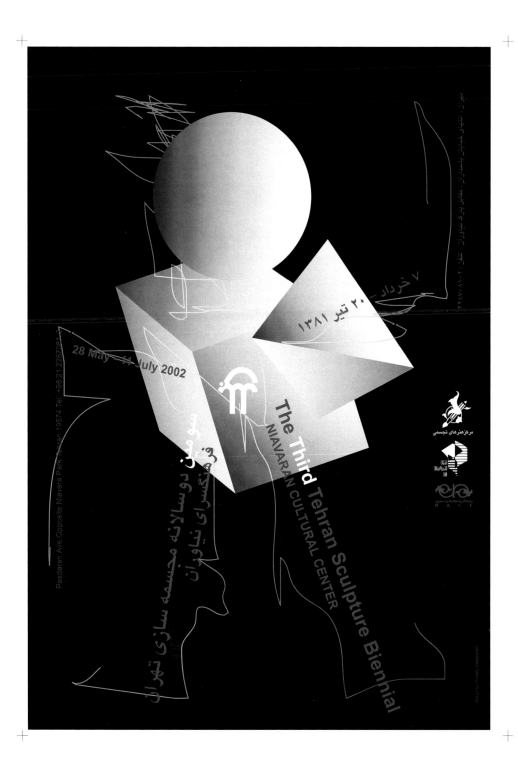

137 **Mostafa Assadollahi**
The Third Tehran Sculpture Biennial
2002

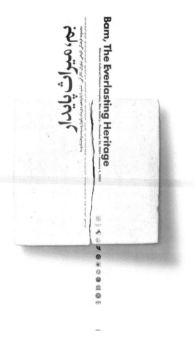

138 **Foad Farahani**
Book 96 / Artists' Book (Exhibition)
2017

139 **Majid Abbasi**
Bam, the Everlasting Heritage
2005

140 **Arad Farhadi**
Autumn 2015 / Vije School of Visual Communications
2015

141 **Mehran Zamani**
Gerhard Richter / A Survey
2004

142 **Foad Farahani**
Book as House
2016

143 **Foad Farahani**
Charsoo / Printmaking Exhibition
2013

144 **Mehdi Mahdian**
The Second International Poster Biennial of the Islamic
World, 2007

145 **Majid Abbasi**
Thousands Sights of Life
2005

146 **Studio Metaphor / Ali Asali**
Unmanned / Mehdi Motazedian (Dian)
2018

147 **ChapChin Studio / Davood Morgan,**
Farid Yahaghi, Javad Zarinia
Tehran Graphic Design Week
2014

Katalog

Alle abgebildeten Plakate stammen aus der Plakatsammlung des Museum für Gestaltung Zürich. Die
Rechte liegen bei den Urheberinnen und Urhebern bzw.
den Rechtsnachfolgerinnen und Rechtsnachfolgern.

Die Daten des Katalogs folgen den Rubriken Gestaltung,
Plakattext, Erscheinungsjahr, Erscheinungsland, Drucktechnik, Format und Donationsnachweis. Dabei gelten
insbesondere folgende Regelungen:

Plakattext: Die beste Textwiedergabe bildet die Abbildung
des Plakates selbst. Darum wird hier eine vereinfachte
Form wiedergegeben, welche nur die aussagekräftigen
Textbestandteile berücksichtigt. Allfällige Umstellungen
dienen der Verständlichkeit. Auf eine Transkription der persischen resp. kyrillischen Schrift wurde verzichtet. Das
Zeichen / trennt inhaltliche Texteinheiten, in Klammern steht
jeweils die Übersetzung.

Erscheinungsland: Das Erscheinungsland wird mit dem
international gebräuchlichen ISO-Code angegeben. Da die
meisten Plakate im Iran im Aushang waren, wird in der
vorliegenden Publikation das Erscheinungsland nur dann
genannt, wenn davon abweichend.

Format: Die Angaben werden in der Abfolge Höhe × Breite
und in cm gemacht. Weil die Plakate oft nicht exakt
rechtwinklig geschnitten sind, werden die Abmessungen
auf halbe cm aufgerundet.

Die Plakatgeschichte ist ein junges Forschungsgebiet –
verlässliche Hinweise sind rar. Jeder Hinweis und jede
Ergänzung sind willkommen:
sammlungen@museum-gestaltung.ch

Catalogue

All posters reproduced are from the Museum für Gestaltung Zürich's Poster Collection. The copyrights are held
by the authors.

The data listed in the catalogue is broken down into the
following sections: designer, poster title and/or text,
year and country of first appearance, printing technique,
size, and donor. In particular, the following rules have
been applied:

Poster text: The poster itself provides the best version
of the text, and thus a simplified form is used which
provides only the most meaningful elements. Any rearrange-
ments that have been made are for purposes of intel-
ligibility. A slash mark separates textual units by content.
A transcription of the Persian or Cyrillic script has been
omitted. The German and/or English translation is set in
parentheses.

Country of first appearance: The country of first
appearance is identified by the internationally accepted
ISO code. Since most of the posters first appeared in
Iran, this publication only notes exceptions.

Format: The dimensions are given in centimeters as
height × width. Because posters are often not cut exactly
at right angles, the dimensions are rounded off to the
half-centimeter.

The history of posters is a recent field of research –
reliable information is rare. Any further references
or additional material are welcome:
sammlungen@museum-gestaltung.ch

1 Morteza Momayez (1935–2005)
Doorguzabad / A Play by Sirus
Ebrahimzadeh
1976 Siebdruck – Screenprint
90,5 × 59 cm
Donation Graphis Verlag, Zürich

2 Mohammadreza Abdolali (*1983)
Sky & Earth / Sculpture Collection
Ghodratollah Agheli / Henna Art
Gallery (Himmel & Erde /
Skulpturensammlung Ghodratollah
Agheli / Henna Art Gallery)
2011 Offset 97 × 68 cm
Donation Mohammadreza Abdolali

3 Ghobad Shiva (*1940)
Festival of Arts Shiraz / Persepolis
1969 Siebdruck – Screenprint
97,5 × 67,5 cm
Donation 5th Color, Teheran

4 Saeid Forootan (*1984)
Theatrical Kiss / A Film by
Karim Lakzadeh
2018 Offset 67,5 × 48,5 cm
Donation Saeid Forootan

5 Studio Kargah /
Sanaz Soltani (*1984)
Arya Tabandehpoor / Corruption,
Retooling, Connection / Mohsen
Gallery (Arya Tabandehpoor /
Manipulation, Umrüstung,
Verbindung / Mohsen Gallery)
2018 Offset 68 × 48,5 cm
Donation Sanaz Soltani

6 Reza Abedini (*1967)
20e Festival international de l'affiche
et du graphisme de Chaumont
FR 2009 Siebdruck – Screenprint
120 × 80 cm
Donation Biennale internationale
de design graphique, Chaumont

7 Majid Abbasi (*1965)
100 Iranian Logotypes / Exhibition
RU 2010 Offset 99 × 69 cm
Donation Majid Abbasi

8 Amir Hossein Ghoochibeik (*1977)
The 3rd International Graphic
Biennial of the Islamic World
2009 Offset 98,5 × 69 cm
Donation Amir Hossein Ghoochibeik

9 Masoud Nejabati (*1967)
The Celebration of Eid al-Ghadir
(Die Feier des Eid al-Ghadir)
2019 Offset 69 × 48,5 cm
Donation Masoud Nejabati

10 Masoud Nejabati (*1967)
The Celebration of the Birth of
Imam Reza (Die Feier der Geburt von
Imam Reza)
2012 Offset 69 × 48,5 cm
Donation Masoud Nejabati

11 Majid Abbasi (*1965)
International Conference on
Masterpieces of the Persian Painting
(Internationale Konferenz über
Meisterwerke der persischen Malerei)
2005 Offset 68 × 48 cm
Donation Majid Abbasi

12 Masoud Nejabati (*1967)
The Celebration of the Birth of
Imam Reza (Die Feier der Geburt
von Imam Reza)
2011 Offset 60 × 45 cm
Donation Masoud Nejabati

13 Mojtaba Adibi (*1988)
Almajoghl Ali Bakhshi / Dutar Playing
for Quchan (Almajoghi Ali Bakhshi
spielt Dotar für Quchan)
2013 Offset 93,5 × 68 cm
Donation Mojtaba Adibi

14 Studio Fa / Mahdi Fatehi (*1982)
The 7th Iranian Folk Music Festival /
Tehran / Kerman
2011 Offset 100 × 70 cm
Donation Mahdi Fatehi

15 Masoud Nejabati (*1967)
Exhibition of Fine Arts / Professors
and Students / Tehran Academy
of Fine Arts
2001 Offset 69,5 × 50 cm
Donation 5th Color, Teheran

16 Studio Kargah /
Peyman Pourhosein (*1980)
The Wedding by Tarlan Rafiee /
Golestan Gallery (Die Hochzeit von
Tarlan Rafiee / Golestan Gallery)
2010 Offset 99 × 68,5 cm
Donation Peyman Pourhosein

17 Mehdi Saeedi (*1979)
The 17th Fadjr International
Music Festival
2002 Offset 98,5 × 68,5 cm
Donation 5th Color, Teheran

18 Mehran Zamani (*1967)
The 1st Fadjr Handicrafts &
Traditional Arts Festival / Iranian
Artists Forum
2017 Offset 100 × 70 cm
Donation Mehran Zamani

19 Mehdi Saeedi (*1979)
14th Fortnight Festival Music
Zekro-Zakarin
2004 Offset 91,5 × 69 cm
Donation 5th Color, Teheran

20 Farzad Adibi (*1967)
Roar of Silent / Khorosh-e-Khamosh /
A Glimpse on Farzad Adibi's
Graphic Art Works (Posters & Book
Covers) / Iranian Artists Forum /
Tehran (Das Brüllen der Stille /
Khorosh-e-Khamosh / Ein Blick
auf Farzad Adibis grafische Arbeiten
(Plakate & Buchumschläge) /
Iranisches Künstlerforum / Teheran)
2007 Offset 100 × 70 cm
Donation Farzad Adibi

21 Reza Babajani (*1981)
2nd Esfand Drawing Annual /
Arteen Art Gallery
2017 Offset 98,5 × 69,5 cm
Donation Reza Babajani

22 Ghobad Shiva (*1940)
5th Festival of Arts Shiraz /
Persepolis
1971 Offset 96 × 67 cm
Donation 5th Color, Teheran

23 Iman Safaei (*1982)
27 April / World Graphics Day
2008 Offset 99 × 69 cm
Donation Iman Safaei

24 Reza Babajani (*1981)
My Soul Is Poured in You /
Painting Group Exhibition / Digari
Art Gallery (Meine Seele ist in
dich geflossen / Malerei-Gruppen-
ausstellung / Digari Art Gallery)
2017 Offset 70 × 49,5 cm
Donation Reza Babajani

25 Mohammad Khodashenas
(*1975)
Götz Gramlich (Germany) /
Toshiyasu Nanbu (Japan) /
Leonardo Sonnoli (Italy) / The Group
Poster Exhibition in Studio
Graphic Design Mohammad
Khodashenas in Lahijan – Iran
2009 Offset 100 × 70 cm
Donation Mohammad Khodashenas

26 Masoud Morgan (*1989)
Knitted Camps / Setare Salehi
Arashloo / Azad Art Gallery
(Gestrickte Lager / Setare Salehi
Arashloo / Azad Art Gallery)
2015 Offset 98 × 68,5 cm
Donation Masoud Morgan

27 Damoon Khanjanzadeh (*1975)
Kambiz Derambakhsh / Tehran
2007 Offset 98 × 68 cm
Donation Damoon Khanjanzadeh

28 Studio Kargah /
Saam Keshmiri (*1986)
Nose to Nose / Slavs and Tatars /
Argo Factory / Pejman Foundation /
The Third Line (Nase an Nase /
Slavs and Tatars / Argo Factory /
Pejman-Stiftung / The Third Line)
2018 Offset 100 × 70 cm
Donation Saam Keshmiri

29 Reza Babajani (*1981)
Ismail Ghanbari / Abandoned /
Azad Art Gallery (Ismail Ghanbari /
Verlassen / Azad Art Gallery)
2016 Offset 98,5 × 68,5 cm
Donation Reza Babajani

30 Majid Kashani (*1978)
Groupage / Photo Group Exhibition /
Silk Road Gallery
2012 Offset 98,5 × 69 cm
Donation Majid Kashani

31 ChapChin Studio / Davood
Morgan (*1982), Javad Zarinia (*1989)
Solo Painting Exhibition /
M. J. Pakravan / Siyavash in Fire /
Ferdowsi Gallery
2018 Offset 69,5 × 48 cm
Donation Davood Morgan,
Javad Zarinia

32 Mohammadreza Abdolali (*1983)
Ghodratollah Agheli / Gradual
Death of a Smile / Azad Art Gallery
(Ghodratollah Agheli / Allmählicher
Tod eines Lächelns / Azad Art
Gallery)
2013 Offset 98,5 × 68,5 cm
Donation Mohammadreza Abdolali

33 Damoon Khanjanzadeh (*1975)
Career Record / Unveiling Karnameh
Publication Typeface (Werdegang /
Vorstellung der Schrift Karnameh)
2012 Offset 98,5 × 69 cm
Donation Damoon Khanjanzadeh

34 Mohammadreza Abdolali (*1983)
Mohsen Mahmoodizade / Protect
Me from What I Want / Azad Art
Gallery (Mohsen Mahmoodizade /
Schütze mich vor dem, was ich will /
Azad Art Gallery)
2015 Offset 98 × 68 cm
Donation Mohammadreza Abdolali

35 Bijan Sayfouri (*1968)
The 5th Color in Cooperation with
Iranian Graphic Designers Society
(IGDS) Presents: Bouf-e kour
(The Blind Owl) / Iranian Typography
Exhibition / Seyhoun Gallery /
Tehran (5th Color in Zusammenarbeit
mit der IGDS präsentiert:
Bouf-e kour (Die blinde Eule) /
Ausstellung iranischer Typografie /
Seyhoun Gallery / Teheran)
2003 Offset 68 × 48 cm
Donation 5th Color, Teheran

36 Bijan Sayfouri (*1968)
Khiyal / The Quarterly Periodical
of the Iranian Academy of the Arts
(Khiyal / Quartalsschrift der
Iranischen Kunstakademie)
2002 Offset 68 × 48 cm
Donation Bijan Sayfouri

37 Mohammad Khodashenas
(*1975)
Hassan Rajabinejad / Photo
Exhibition
2006 Offset 68,5 × 97,5 cm
Donation Mohammad Khodashenas

38 Studio Metaphor / Ali Asali (*1988)
Narges Mousavi / Angels Over
Tehran / Azad Art Gallery
(Narges Mousavi / Engel über
Teheran / Azad Art Gallery)
2015 Offset 98 × 68 cm
Donation Ali Asali

39 Studio Kargah /
Aria Kasaei (*1980)
Graphic Design Week Tehran 09 /
Urban Design
2009 Offset 98 × 68 cm
Donation Aria Kasaei

40 Studio Metaphor / Ali Asali (*1988)
Folding / Amir Farsijani /
Azad Art Gallery (Auffaltung /
Amir Farsijani / Azad Art Gallery)
2016 Offset 98,5 × 68,5 cm
Donation Ali Asali

41 Studio Kargah /
Aria Kasaei (*1980)
The Nest Has Been Destroyed /
Curated by Gaia Serena Simionati /
Azad Art Gallery (Das Nest wurde
zerstört / Kuratiert von Gaia Serena
Simionati / Azad Art Gallery)
2011 Offset 98 × 68 cm
Donation Aria Kasaei

42 Morteza Mahallati (1970–2020)
Rokhsat Poster Exhibition /
Vessal Shirazi Gallery
2008 Offset 97,5 × 69,5 cm
Donation Morteza Mahallati

43 Studio Fa / Mahdi Fatehi (*1982)
New York / Tehran /
Group Street Art Exhibition /
Seyhoun Art Gallery
2014 Offset 100 × 70 cm
Donation Mahdi Fatehi

44 Reza Babajani (*1981)
A Man with the Flower in His Mouth /
The Hall of Ferdowsi University of
Mashhad (Ein Mann mit einer Blume
im Mund / Konferenzsaal der
Firdausi-Universität Maschhad)
2009 Offset 100 × 68 cm
Donation Reza Babajani

45 Studio Kargah /
Aria Kasaei (*1980)
Bimzar / Azad Art Gallery
2010 Offset 98 × 68 cm
Donation Aria Kasaei

46 Reza Abedini (*1967)
Mehran Mohajer / Reza Abedini /
Photo + Graphic Exhibition /
Marlik Art Gallery
2004 Offset 70 × 46 cm
Donation Reza Abedini

47 Pedram Harby (*1977)
Urban Art House Presents: Tehran
I Love You / Photography Group
Exhibition / Curated by: Namdar
Shirazian / Sabz Gallery (Urban Art
House präsentiert: Teheran, ich
liebe dich / Fotografie-Gruppenaus-
stellung / Kuratiert von Namdar
Shirazian / Sabz Gallery)
2013 Offset 68 × 47,5 cm
Donation Pedram Harby

48 Bijan Sayfouri (*1968)
The 13th Tehran International
Book Fair
2000 Offset 67 × 48 cm
Donation 5th Color, Teheran

49 Pedram Harby (*1977)
An Evening of Theater / The Fifth
Chapter / Staged Readings
(Ein Theaterabend / Das fünfte
Kapitel / Szenische Lesungen)
1999 Offset 68 × 48,5 cm
Donation 5th Color, Teheran

50 Majid Abbasi (*1965)
A Mieczysław Wasilewski
Retrospective in Tehran /
Exhibition, Lecture & Workshop /
Imam Ali Religious Arts Museum
2007 Offset 70 × 49 cm
Donation Majid Abbasi

51 ChapChin Studio / Davood Morgan (*1982), Javad Zarinia (*1989) Farzad Annual / Contemporary Drawing / Farzad Art Gallery (Farzad-Jahresausstellung / Zeitgenössische Zeichnung / Farzad Art Gallery) 2017 Offset 48 × 33,5 cm Donation Davood Morgan, Javad Zarinia

52 Studio Metaphor / Ali Asali (*1988) Tadaex / 6th Tehran Annual Digital Art Exhibition / Tadagrant 2016 / International Open Call 2016 Offset 98,5 × 68,5 cm Donation Ali Asali

53 Studio Kargah / Peyman Pourhosein (*1980) Plakart / On Iranian Cinema Marquee Posters / Salam Art Gallery (Plakart / Herausragende iranische Kinoplakate / Salam Art Gallery) 2017 Offset 68 × 99 cm Donation Peyman Pourhosein

54 Studio Kargah / Peyman Pourhosein (*1980) Cold Fire / An Overview of Photographs from the Iran-Iraq War / Salam Art Gallery (Kaltes Feuer / Ein Überblick über Fotografien aus dem Ersten Golfkrieg / Salam Art Gallery) 2018 Offset 68 × 99 cm Donation Peyman Pourhosein

55 Studio Kargah / Aria Kasaei (*1980) Chasm / Malek Foundation (Kluft / Malek Foundation) 2019 Offset 99,5 × 60 cm Donation Aria Kasaei

56 Morteza Momayez (1935–2005) Hommage an Pablo Neruda / Chilenische Woche 80 / Gestaltung und Entwurf «Morteza Momayez» (Tribute to Pablo Neruda / 80th Chilean Week / Design and Sketch "Morteza Momayez") DE 1980 Siebdruck – Screenprint 100 × 70 cm Donation Morteza Momayez

57 Morteza Momayez (1935–2005) Exhibition of Graphic Works / Morteza Momayez ca. 1975 Siebdruck – Screenprint 86,5 × 57,5 cm Donation Graphis Verlag, Zürich

58 Morteza Momayez (1935–2005) Film Market / IVth Tehran International Film Festival 1975 Siebdruck – Screenprint 89 × 58 cm Donation Graphis Verlag, Zürich

59 Ebrahim Haghighi (*1949) Andrzej Wajda / Images of an Era / 7th Fajr International Film Festival (Andrzej Wajda / Bilder einer Ära / 7. Internationales Fajr-Filmfestival) 1989 Siebdruck – Screenprint 69,5 × 43,5 cm Donation Graphis Verlag, Zürich

60 Shahab Tondar (*1987) Painting Exhibition by Amirpasha Hoshivar / Silk Road Gallery 2010 Offset 70 × 50 cm Donation Shahab Tondar

61 Morteza Momayez (1935–2005) Hommage an Pablo Neruda / Chilenische Woche 80 / Gestaltung und Entwurf «Morteza Momayez» (Tribute to Pablo Neruda / 80th Chilean Week / Design and Sketch "Mortoza Momayez") DE 1980 Siebdruck – Screenprint 100 × 70 cm Donation Morteza Momayez

62 Morteza Momayez (1935–2005) Photo: Ali Khosravi Buster Keaton: The Sentimental Face / Vth Tehran International Film Festival (Buster Keaton: Das sentimentale Gesicht / 5. Internationales Filmfestival Teheran) 1976 Siebdruck – Screenprint 86 × 60 cm Donation Graphis Verlag, Zürich

63 Mohammad Reza Dadgar (*1949) Blind War / The Institute for the Intellectual Development of Children and Young Adults / Tehran (Blinder Krieg / Institut für die intellektuelle Entwicklung von Kindern und jungen Erwachsenen) 1979 Siebdruck – Screenprint 70 × 49,5 cm Donation Graphis Verlag, Zürich

64 Studio Kargah / Saam Keshmiri (*1986) Celebrating the Centenary of Tehran Music Academy (Feierlichkeiten zum hundert-jährigen Bestehen der Teheraner Musikakademie) 2019 Offset 99 × 68,5 cm Donation Saam Keshmiri

65 Ghobad Shiva (*1940) 800th Anniversary of the Birth of Saadi, Iranian Thinker, Poet and Writer (800. Geburtstag von Saadi, iranischer Denker, Dichter und Schriftsteller) 1984 Offset 66 × 48,5 cm Donation 5th Color, Teheran

66 Alireza Mostafazadeh Ebrahimi (*1962) Nature Invites Us to Graphic Art. Graphic Art Invites Us to Nature. (Die Natur inspiriert uns zur Grafik. Die Grafik inspiriert uns zur Natur.) 2003 Offset, Siebdruck – Screenprint 98,5 × 68,5 cm Donation 5th Color, Teheran

67 Alireza Mostafazadeh Ebrahimi (*1962) Antigone / Zaman Theater Group 2009 Offset 69 × 48,5 cm Donation Alireza Mostafazadeh Ebrahimi

68 Alireza Mostafazadeh Ebrahimi (*1962) Hello and Goodbye / by: Athol Fugard / Director: Hooshmand Honarkar 2012 Offset 69 × 48,5 cm Donation Alireza Mostafazadeh Ebrahimi

69 Alireza Mostafazadeh Ebrahimi (*1962) What Twisted the Father's Mustache (Was dem Vater den Schnurrbart verdrehte) 2014 Offset 69 × 48 cm Donation Alireza Mostafazadeh Ebrahimi

70 Sadegh Barirani (*1923) Coppelia / Music by: Leo Delibes / Iranian National Ballet Company / Roudaki Hall 1971 Siebdruck – Screenprint 82 × 50,5 cm

71 Mojtaba Adibi (*1988) King Lear / Maaa Theater / New York and Tehran 2017 Offset 68 × 49 cm Donation Mojtaba Adibi

72 Siamak Pourjabbar (*1976) Anti-Gone / Iranshahr Theater / Tehran 2018 Offset 69 × 48,5 cm Donation Siamak Pourjabbar

73 Farshid Mesghali (*1943) Children Literature in the Service of International Understanding and Peaceful Co-Operation (Kinderliteratur im Dienst der Völkerverständigung und der friedlichen Zusammenarbeit) 1975 Offset 69 × 49 cm Donation 5th Color, Teheran

74 Alireza Mostafazadeh Ebrahimi (*1962)
Once Upon a Time, Playing
(Es war einmal, als wir spielten)
2012 Offset 69 × 48 cm
Donation Alireza Mostafazadeh Ebrahimi

75 Farshid Mesghali (*1943)
Polish Animation Films / 11th Tehran International Festival of Films for Children and Young Adults
1976 Siebdruck – Screenprint 99,5 × 69,5 cm
Donation Graphis Verlag, Zürich

76 Homa Delvaray (*1980)
Divarkoob / 49 Posters of 51 Graphic Designers / Poster Exhibition
2010 Offset 98,5 × 68,5 cm
Donation Homa Delvaray

77 Amirali Ghasemi (*1980)
Urban Jealousy / The 1st Intl. Roaming Biennial of Tehran / Kentsel Kıskançlık / Hafriyat Karakoy (Urbane Eifersucht / 1. Internationale Wanderbiennale Teheran / Kentsel Kıskançlık / Hafriyat Karakoy)
2008 Offset 100,5 × 70,5 cm
Donation Amirali Ghasemi

78 Siamak Pourjabbar (*1976)
Side by Side in Solidarity / Greeting from Iran / Japan Earthquake, Tsunami & Nuclear Crisis 2011 (Seite an Seite in Solidarität / Grüsse aus dem Iran / Erdbeben in Japan, Tsunami & Nuklear-katastrophe 2011)
2011 Offset 100 × 70 cm
Donation Siamak Pourjabbar

79 Amirali Ghasemi (*1980)
Urban Jealousy in Berlin / The 1st Intl. Roaming Biennial of Tehran / Kentsel Kıskançlık (Urbane Eifer-sucht in Berlin / 1. Internationale Wanderbiennale Teheran / Kentsel Kıskançlık)
2008 Offset 98 × 69 cm
Donation Amirali Ghasemi

80 Homa Delvaray (*1980)
Tehran Monoxide Project / Photos from Four-to-Eighteen-Year-Olds' Viewpoint / Manzoumeh Kherad Institute (Tehran Monoxide Project / Fotos aus der Sicht von Vier- bis Achtzehnjährigen / Manzoumeh Kherad Institute)
2014 Offset 98 × 68 cm
Donation Homa Delvaray

81 Mehrzad Dirin (*1981)
27th Fajr Music Festival
2012 Offset 68 × 67,5 cm
Donation Mehrzad Dirin

82 Mehrzad Dirin (*1981)
11th Shiraz Fajr Film Festival
2012 Offset 68 × 68 cm
Donation Mehrzad Dirin

83 Mehrzad Dirin (*1981)
4th Shiraz Today International Photo Festival
2017 Offset 90 × 62 cm
Donation Mehrzad Dirin

84 Majid Abbasi (*1965)
Streets of Tehran / A Selection of Mahmoud Pakzad's Photographs / Mirmiran Gallery (Strassen von Teheran / Eine Auswahl der Fotografien von Mahmoud Pakzad / Mirmiran Gallery)
2006 Offset 70 × 49 cm
Donation Majid Abbasi

85 Mohammad Khodashenas (*1975)
Samira Eskandarfar / There Is No Us / Azad Art Gallery (Samira Eskandarfar / Es gibt kein Wir / Azad Art Gallery)
2019 Offset 97,5 × 68,5 cm
Donation Mohammad Khodashenas

86 ChapChin Studio / Davood Morgan (*1982), Farid Yahaghi (*1983)
Photo: Aghil Hosseinian (*1990)
World Urbanism Day / Research Center of Ministry of Housing and Urban Development / Tehran (Welttag der Stadtplanung / Forschungszentrum des Ministeriums für Wohnungsbau und Stadtentwicklung / Teheran)
2013 Offset 67,5 × 48 cm
Donation Davood Morgan, Farid Yahaghi

87 Alireza Mostafazadeh Ebrahimi (*1962)
Houshang Golshiri / Prince Ehtejab / First Memorial Service for Golshiri (Houshang Golshiri / Prinz Ehtejab / Erste Gedenkfeier für Golshiri)
2001 Offset 67 × 47,5 cm
Donation 5th Color, Teheran

88 Mojtaba Adibi (*1988)
Khat-e Khati / Abousaeed Eskandari / Maan Art Gallery
2019 Offset 68 × 49 cm
Donation Mojtaba Adibi

89 Siamak Pourjabbar (*1976)
Greed / Homa Art Gallery (Gier / Homa Art Gallery)
2012 Offset 69,5 × 48,5 cm
Donation Siamak Pourjabbar

90 Mehran Zamani (*1967)
The 14th Tehran International Ritual-Traditional Theatre Festival
2009 Offset 97,5 × 69 cm
Donation Mehran Zamani

91 Studio Kargah / Saam Keshmiri (*1986)
Homarg / Album by Baramant
2019 Offset 50 × 35 cm
Donation Saam Keshmiri

92 Majid Kashani (*1978)
The Sound of One Hand / Honar Hall (Der Klang einer Hand / Honar Hall)
2013 Offset 70 × 49,5 cm
Donation Majid Kashani

93 Studio Kargah / Sanaz Soltani (*1984)
Land / Ali Phi / Mohsen Gallery
2017 Offset 69 × 49 cm
Donation Sanaz Soltani

94 Shahab Tondar (*1987)
The Years of Fire and Blood (Die Jahre des Feuers und des Blutes)
2020 Offset 49 × 33,5 cm
Donation Shahab Tondar

95 Studio Kargah / Sanaz Soltani (*1984)
Home / Gohar Dashti / Mohsen Gallery
2017 Offset 69 × 48,5 cm
Donation Sanaz Soltani

96 Iman Safaei (*1982)
Ramtin Zad / Painting Exhibition / Golestan Gallery / Tehran
2007 Offset 98,5 × 68,5 cm
Donation Iman Safaei

97 Studio Kargah / Peyman Pourhosein (*1980)
The International Congress of Shiraz School
2008 Offset 48,5 × 69 cm
Donation Peyman Pourhosein

98 Studio Kargah / Peyman Pourhosein (*1980)
Horses Stomp at the Window 1 / Vahdat Hall / Tehran (Pferde stampfen vor dem Fenster 1 / Vahdat Hall / Teheran)
2011 Offset 68,5 × 99,5 cm
Donation Peyman Pourhosein

99 Morteza Akoochekian (*1981)
Tehran; Lorzadeh / The Architect House-Museum
2019 Offset 68,5 × 48,5 cm
Donation Morteza Akoochekian

100 Morteza Akoochekian (*1981)
Settimana del cinema italiano /
La casa degli artisti (Italienische
Filmwoche / Iranisches Künstler-
forum – Italian Film Week / Iranian
Artists Forum)
2018 Offset 68,5 × 49 cm
Donation Morteza Akoochekian

101 Morteza Akoochekian (*1981)
Khayyam / Millennium Anniversary /
Niavaran Cultural Center
2018 Offset 68,5 × 49 cm
Donation Morteza Akoochekian

102 Amirali Ghasemi (*1980)
Drawer / Visual Snippets of
"Chargoosh" / Laleh Art Gallery
(Schublade / Visuelle Schnipsel von
«Chargoosh» / Laleh Art Gallery)
2007 Offset 100 × 69,5 cm
Donation Amirali Ghasemi

103 Studio Kargah /
Masoud Morgan (*1989)
Mostafa Jafari / Gunshots in the
Eyes of Spirits / Azad Art Gallery
(Mostafa Jafari / Schüsse in
die Augen von Geistern / Azad Art
Gallery)
2011 Offset 98 × 67,5 cm
Donation Masoud Morgan

104 Pedram Harby (*1977)
Urban Art House Presents:
Third Tehran Fusion Music Week /
Niavaran Cultural Center
2016 Offset 68 × 49 cm
Donation Pedram Harby

105 Ebrahim Haghighi (*1949)
A Persian Requiem / Simin
Daneshvar (Drama der Trauer /
Simin Daneschwar)
2001 Offset 69 × 48 cm
Donation 5th Color, Teheran

106 Ebrahim Haghighi (*1949)
Me, Taraneh / 15 Years Old /
Milad Film Tehran (Ich, Taraneh /
15 Jahre alt / Milad Film Teheran)
2002 Offset 99 × 68 cm
Donation 5th Color, Teheran

107 Masoud Nejabati (*1967)
Exhibition of Fine Arts by
Professors and Students /
Academy of Fine Arts for Young
Men / Arasbaran Cultural Center /
Tehran
2002 Offset 67 × 48 cm
Donation 5th Color, Teheran

108 Saed Meshki (*1964)
The 3rd International Theatre
Festival of Iranzamin
2001 Offset 68 × 48 cm
Donation 5th Color, Teheran

109 Mehdi Saeedi (*1979)
The 19th Fadjr International
Music Festival
2004 Offset 94,5 × 67 cm
Donation 5th Color, Teheran

110 Reza Abedini (*1967)
The 23rd Fadjr International
Theater Festival / Tehran
2005 Offset 98 × 68 cm
Donation Reza Abedini

111 Reza Abedini (*1967)
Painting Exhibition / Rezvan
Sadeghzadeh / Golestan Gallery
2005 Offset 97,5 × 68,5 cm
Donation Reza Abedini

112 Reza Abedini (*1967)
AllOne / Reza Abedini / Vije Gallery
2006 Offset 96,5 × 68 cm
Donation Reza Abedini

113 Studio Kargah /
Sanaz Soltani (*1984)
Skin, Flesh, and Bone / Arya
Tabandehpoor / Mohsen Gallery
(Haut, Fleisch und Knochen /
Arya Tabandehpoor / Mohsen
Gallery)
2017 Offset 69 × 49 cm
Donation Sanaz Soltani

114 Reza Abedini (*1967)
Siah Mashq / Reza Abedini's Posters
2004 Offset 98 × 68 cm
Donation Reza Abedini

115 Saed Meshki (*1964)
Third Film Festival in Memory of
the Abadan Uprising / A Tribute to
Nasser Taghvai (Drittes Filmfestival
in Erinnerung an den Abadan-
Aufstand / Hommage an Nasser
Taghvai)
2002 Offset 68,5 × 47,5 cm
Donation 5th Color, Teheran

116 Saeid Forootan (*1984)
The Redhead / A Film by: Karim
Lakzadeh / Producer: Mehdi Rashidi
2017 Offset 67,5 × 48,5 cm
Donation Saeid Forootan

117 Pedram Harby (*1977)
Final Encore II / Dastan's Basement /
Curated by: Sogol Kashani /
Joubeen Mireskandari / Shahin
Armin (Letzte Zugabe II / Dastans
Keller / Kuratiert von Sogol Kashani /
Joubeen Mireskandari / Shahin
Armin)
2013 Offset 69 × 48 cm
Donation Pedram Harby

118 Ali Khorshidpour (*1964)
Assemblage Art / Introducing
French Contemporary Artist Arman /
Tehran Museum of Contemporary
Art (Assemblage-Kunst / Vorstellung
des zeitgenössischen französischen
Künstlers Arman / Museum für
zeitgenössische Kunst Teheran)
2003 Offset 67,5 × 48 cm
Donation 5th Color, Teheran

119 Pedram Harby (*1977)
Where Were You on January 8th? /
by Amir Reza Koohestani (Wo warst
du am 8. Januar? / Von Amir Reza
Koohestani)
2009 Offset 69 × 50 cm
Donation Pedram Harby

120 Pedram Harby (*1977)
Mehr Theatre Group Presents:
Ivanov / Iranshahr Theater
2011 Offset 48 × 68,5 cm
Donation Pedram Harby

121 Majid Abbasi (*1965)
. . . in Memory of Kaveh Golestan
(. . . in Erinnerung an Kaveh
Golestan)
2003 Offset 100,5 × 69,5 cm
Donation 5th Color, Teheran

122 Majid Abbasi (*1965)
An Exhibition of the Photographs
(Original Prints) of Sadeq Hedayat /
Seyhoun Gallery (Fotoausstellung
(Originalabzüge) von Sadeq
Hedayat / Seyhoun Gallery)
2001 Offset 70 × 50 cm
Donation Majid Abbasi

123 Farzad Adibi (*1967)
Monthly Journal of Literature
and Philosophy / Khaneh Ketab /
Tehran
2002 Offset, Siebdruck –
Screenprint 68 × 48 cm
Donation 5th Color, Teheran

124 Morteza Momayez (1935–2005)
Ali Nassirian in: The Custodian /
A Film by Khosrow Haritash
1976 Siebdruck – Screenprint
88 × 55 cm
Donation Graphis Verlag, Zürich

125 Reza Abedini (*1967)
Reza Abedini / Complexion /
Virtual Poster Exhibition! Momayez
Gallery (Reza Abedini / Erschei-
nungsbild / Virtuelle Plakat-
ausstellung! Momayez Gallery)
2005 Offset 98,5 × 68,5 cm
Donation Reza Abedini

126 Reza Abedini (*1967)
Reza Afsari / Painting Exhibition /
Azad Art Gallery
2009 Offset 98,5 × 68,5 cm
Donation Reza Abedini

127 Reza Abedini (*1967)
Raha Rastifard / I & … /
Azad Art Gallery (Raha Rastifard /
Ich & … / Azad Art Gallery)
2011 Offset 98 × 68,5 cm
Donation Reza Abedini

128 Reza Abedini (*1967)
Parastou Forouhar / I Surrender /
Azad Art Gallery (Parastou Forouhar /
Ich ergebe mich / Azad Art Gallery)
2009 Offset 98 × 68,5 cm
Donation Reza Abedini

129 Reza Abedini (*1967)
Book Presentation / Dabireh: Alef /
A Journal of Persian Type and
Language / An Attempt of Dabireh
Collective / Exhibition: Old Religious
Posters from Parviz Tanavoli's
Private Collection / Iranian Artists
Forum (Buchvorstellung / Dabireh:
Alef / Eine Zeitschrift für persische
Schrift und Sprache / Ein Versuch
des Dabireh-Kollektivs / Ausstellung:
Alte religiöse Plakate aus der
Privatsammlung von Parviz Tanavoli /
Iranisches Künstlerforum)
2009 Offset 98,5 × 68 cm
Donation Reza Abedini

130 Reza Abedini (*1967)
Hossein Maher / Painting
Exhibition / Assar Art Gallery
2007 Offset 98 × 68 cm
Donation Reza Abedini

131 Reza Abedini (*1967)
Sirak Melkonian / Azad Art Gallery
2008 Offset 98,5 × 68 cm
Donation Reza Abedini

132 Reza Babajani (*1981)
Javad Modaresi Havas / Black
Forest II / Azad Art Gallery (Javad
Modaresi Havas / Schwarzer
Wald II / Azad Art Gallery)
2017 Offset 98,5 × 68,5 cm
Donation Reza Babajani

133 Pedram Harby (*1977)
Choir: Our Legacy, Fades and Melts
Away, Because Tomorrow May
Not Ever Be / The Performance Art /
Parham Taghioff / Actors: Milad
Mapar, Nima Moheb (Chor: Unser
Vermächtnis, vergeht und schmilzt
dahin, weil es vielleicht nie ein Morgen
gibt / Performance-Kunst / Parham
Taghioff / Schauspielerinnen/Schau-
spieler: Milad Mapar, Nima Moheb)
2003 Offset 68,5 × 49 cm
Donation 5th Color, Teheran

134 Pedram Harby (*1977)
Installation / Arash Yadollahi
2001 Offset 68,5 × 48,5 cm
Donation 5th Color, Teheran

135 Pedram Harby (*1977)
I'm Not a Story You Can Tell,
I'm Not a Song You Can Sing,
I'm Not a Voice You Can Hear or
Something You Can See or
Something You Can Know…
(Ich bin keine Geschichte, die man
erzählen kann, ich bin kein Lied,
das man singen kann, ich bin keine
Stimme, die man hören kann,
oder etwas, das man sehen oder
etwas, das man wissen kann…)
1999 Offset 68 × 49 cm
Donation 5th Color, Teheran

136 Iman Safaei (*1982)
Sculptures by Jolee / Julie /
Sculpture Exhibition by Hassan
Razghandi
2007 Offset 99 × 68,5 cm
Donation Iman Safaei

137 Mostafa Assadollahi (*1950)
The Third Tehran Sculpture Biennial /
Niavaran Cultural Center
2002 Offset 69 × 48 cm
Donation 5th Color, Teheran

138 Foad Farahani (*1982)
Book 96 / Artists' Book
(Exhibition) / Aaran Gallery
2017 Offset 68 × 49 cm
Donation Foad Farahani

139 Majid Abbasi (*1965)
Bam, the Everlasting Heritage /
Niavaran Cultural/Historic Complex,
Blue Gallery (Bam, das ewige
Vermächtnis / Kulturhistorischer
Komplex von Niavaran, Blue Gallery)
2005 Offset 97,5 × 68 cm
Donation Majid Abbasi

140 Arad Farhadi (*1982)
Autumn 2015 / Vije School of
Visual Communications / Tehran
2015 Offset 48 × 33 cm
Donation Arad Farhadi

141 Mehran Zamani (*1967)
Gerhard Richter / A Survey / Tehran
Museum of Contemporary Art
(Gerhard Richter / Ein Überblick /
Museum für zeitgenössische Kunst
Teheran)
2004 Offset 86,5 × 57,5 cm
Donation Mehran Zamani

142 Foad Farahani (*1982)
Book as House / Aaran Projects /
Curated by Foad Farahani /
Aaran Gallery (Das Buch als Haus /
Aaran Projekte / Kuratiert von
Foad Farahani / Aaran Gallery)
2016 Offset 68 × 48 cm
Donation Foad Farahani

143 Foad Farahani (*1982)
Charsoo / Printmaking Exhibition /
Haft-samar Gallery (Charsoo /
Druckgrafikausstellung / Haft-samar
Gallery)
2013 Offset 98,5 × 69 cm
Donation Foad Farahani

144 Mehdi Mahdian (*1980)
The Second International Poster
Biennial of the Islamic World /
Iranian Academy of Art / Saba
Cultural and Artistic Institute
2007 Offset 98,5 × 69 cm
Donation Mehdi Mahdian

145 Majid Abbasi (*1965)
Thousands Sights of Life / Exhibition
of Photographs of Ernst Hoeltzer
from Naser al-Din Shah's Age /
Saba Gallery (Tausend Ansichten
des Lebens / Ausstellung der
Fotografien von Ernst Hoeltzer aus
der Zeit von Naser al-Din Schah /
Saba Gallery)
2005 Offset 84,5 × 59 cm
Donation Majid Abbasi

146 Studio Metaphor / Ali Asali (*1988)
Unmanned / Mehdi Motazedian
(Dian) / Azad Art Gallery
2018 Offset 98 × 68,5 cm
Donation Ali Asali

147 ChapChin Studio / Davood
Morgan (*1982), Farid Yahaghi
(*1983), Javad Zarinia (*1989)
Photo: Aghil Hosseinian (*1990),
Hossein Shirvani
Tehran Graphic Design Week /
Iran Artists Forum
2014 Offset 97,5 × 67,5 cm
Donation Davood Morgan,
Farid Yahaghi, Javad Zarinia

Ausgewählte Literatur / Selected Bibliography

Abedini, Reza, Hans Wolbers (eds.), *New Visual Culture of Modern Iran,* New York 2006.

Amanat, Abbas, *Iran: A Modern History,* New Haven / London 2017.

Hill, Peter Thomas, Gregory Vines (eds.), *Iranian Typography: 50 Years of Calligraphy and Typography in Iranian Graphic Design,* Tehran 2007.

Iranian Graphic Designers Society (ed.), *Iranian Posters from Imagery to Typography: The First Iranian Graphic Design and Typography Exhibition in Russia,* Tehran 2004.

L. A. Mayer Museum for Islamic Art (ed.), *Sign from Iran: Contemporary Iranian Posters. From the Collection of the Moravian Gallery, Brno, Czech Republic,* Jerusalem 2016.

Le Quernec, Alain (ed.), *Reza Abedini,* Design & Designer 026, Paris 2004.

Neshan, nos. 1–47, Tehran 2003–2020, www.neshanmagazine.com/About.aspx?I=2.

Radio Zones (ed.), *Un cri persan,* exh. cat. Salon du livre de Genève, Geneva 2008.

Shehab, Bahia, Haytham Nawar, *A History of Arab Graphic Design,* Cairo 2020.

Téhéran Institut du Développement des Arts Plastiques (ed.), *Un cri persan: Exposition des graphistes Iraniens,* exh. cat. Les Silos, maison du livre et de l'affiche, Chaumont, Tehran 2003.

www.artmag.ir/en/mortezamomayez

www.grapheine.com/en/graphic-design-en/graphic-design-in-iran-persian-heritage-and-modernity

www.grapheine.com/en/history-of-graphic-design/reza-abedini-father-of-iranian-contemporary-graphic-design

www.stirworld.com/think-opinions-graphic-design-in-iran-a-journey-of-evolution-and-practices-shaping-the-future

www.theicod.org/en/resources/news-archive/contemporary-graphic-design-of-iran

Autorinnen und Autoren / Authors

Bettina Richter
Geboren 1964 in Basel, Kunsthistorikerin. 1996 Dissertation über die Antikriegsgrafiken von Théophile-Alexandre Steinlen. 1997–2006 wissenschaftliche Mitarbeiterin in der Plakatsammlung des Museum für Gestaltung Zürich. Seit 2006 Kuratorin der Plakatsammlung. Nebenbei Tätigkeit als Dozentin an der Zürcher Hochschule der Künste sowie als freischaffende Autorin.

Born in 1964 in Basel, art historian. 1996 dissertation on the antiwar graphics of Théophile-Alexandre Steinlen. From 1997 to 2006, served as a research associate for the Poster Collection of the Museum für Gestaltung Zürich, since 2006 as its curator. Also lectures at the Zurich University of the Arts and works as a freelance writer.

Majid Abbasi
1965 in Teheran geboren. Studium der Visuellen Kommunikation an der Fakultät für Bildende Kunst der Universität Teheran. Chefdesigner bei Studio Abbasi, einer international tätigen Agentur für Grafikdesign mit Büros in Teheran und Toronto. Majid Abbasi leitet eine Vielzahl von Designprojekten für Start-ups, Non-Profit-Organisationen und kulturelle Einrichtungen. Als Dozent, Jurymitglied, Kurator und Autor spielt er eine aktive Rolle in der internationalen Designszene. Von 2010 bis 2020 war Abbasi zudem Chefredakteur von *Neshan,* dem führenden iranischen Magazin für Grafikdesign. Er ist Mitglied der Iranian Graphic Designers Society (IGDS) und der Alliance Graphique Internationale (AGI).

Born in 1965 in Tehran. Studied visual communications at the Faculty of Fine Arts, University of Tehran. He is the design director of Studio Abbasi, active in the international community, based in Tehran and Toronto. Abbasi leads a variety of design projects for start-ups, nonprofits, and cultural institutions. He actively contributes to the international design scene as an instructor, jury member, curator, and writer. From 2010 to 2020 he was editor-in-chief of *Neshan,* the leading Iranian graphic design magazine. Abbasi is a member of the Iranian Graphic Designers Society (IGDS) and Alliance Graphique Internationale (AGI).

Maryam Razi
1990 in Schiras geboren. Von 2009 bis 2012 studierte Maryam Razi Visuelle Kommunikation am Shiraz Art Institute of Higher Education. 2016 machte sie an der Alzahra University einen Masterabschluss in Art Research. Razi ist Autorin, Grafikdesignerin, freie Kuratorin und angehende Brillendesignerin. Derzeit arbeitet sie mit dem UCLA Art|Sci Center + Lab in Los Angeles zusammen.

Born in 1990 in Shiraz. Studied Visual Communication at Shiraz Art Institute of Higher Education, 2009–12. MA in Art Research from Alzahra University, 2016. Razi is a writer, graphic designer, independent curator, and eyewear craftswoman in the making. She is currently collaborating with the UCLA Art|Sci Center + Lab in Los Angeles.

Dank / Acknowledgments

Publikations- und Ausstellungsprojekte sind immer ein willkommener Anlass, den eigenen umfangreichen Bestand an Plakaten themenspezifisch zu sichten, aufzuarbeiten und zu ergänzen. Für die vorliegende Publikation konnten wir auf viele iranische Plakate zurückgreifen, die die Sammlung seit der Jahrtausendwende bereichert haben. Insbesondere ist auf die umfangreiche Donation aus dem Jahr 2004 von 5th Color zu verweisen, ein Zusammenschluss von vier Grafikern, die sich der Förderung und Verbreitung des iranischen Plakats verpflichtet haben. 2021 gingen rund 200 neue, zeitgenössische Plakate als Donation von iranischen Grafikerinnen und Grafikern in die Sammlung ein, die von Majid Abbasi zusammengetragen wurden.

Für das uns geschenkte Vertrauen möchten wir uns an dieser Stelle ganz herzlich bedanken. Besonderer Dank gebührt Majid Abbasi, der nicht nur die jüngste Donation verantwortet, sondern uns mit Hinweisen, Erklärungen und Übersetzungen zur Seite stand und für die vorliegende Publikation einen Essay beigetragen hat. Ebenfalls danken wir Mohsen Rahimi, der uns mit weiteren Übersetzungen und Erläuterungen zu ausgewählten Plakaten unterstützt hat. Dem Freundeskreis des Museum für Gestaltung Zürich ist es schliesslich zu verdanken, dass alle Plakate zügig erfasst und fotografiert werden konnten.

Publication and exhibition projects always provide a welcome opportunity to sift through our own extensive poster inventory on a specific subject and to supplement it with new works. For this publication, we were able to draw on a rich trove of Iranian posters that have augmented the collection since the turn of the millennium. Particularly noteworthy is a large donation in 2004 from 5th Color, an alliance of four graphic designers who are committed to raising awareness of the Iranian poster. In 2021, the collection then acquired some two hundred new contemporary posters by Iranian graphic designers, assembled by Majid Abbasi.

We would like to express our sincere gratitude for being entrusted with these works. Special thanks in particular to Majid Abbasi, who is not only responsible for the most recent donation but has also assisted us by contributing references, explanations, and translations, as well as an essay for this publication. Our thanks go as well to Mohsen Rahimi, who provided us with further translations and explanations of selected posters. And we would also like to recognize the Circle of Friends of the Museum für Gestaltung Zürich for making it possible through its support to rapidly catalogue and photograph all of the posters.

Museum für Gestaltung Zürich

Eine Publikation des Museum für Gestaltung Zürich Christian Brändle, Direktor

A Publication of the Museum für Gestaltung Zürich Christian Brändle, Director

Contemporary Iran
Konzept und Redaktion / Concept and editing: Bettina Richter, Petra Schmid, Nico Lazúla
Gestaltung / Design: Integral Lars Müller
Übersetzung / Translation: Antoinette Aichele-Platen (Eng.–Ger.), Abdollah Ghareh Baghi (Pers.–Eng.), Mohsen Rahimi (Pers.–Ger.), Jennifer Taylor (Ger.–Eng.)
Lektorat Deutsch / German copyediting: Markus Zehentbauer
Lektorat Englisch / English copyediting: Jonathan Fox
Fotografie / Photography: Roland Regner, Ivan Šuta
Lithografie / Repro: prints professional, Berlin, Germany
Druck, Einband / Printing, binding: Belvédère, Oosterbeek, The Netherlands

Reihe / Series «Poster Collection»
Herausgegeben von / Edited by
Museum für Gestaltung Zürich, Plakatsammlung
Bettina Richter, Kuratorin der Plakatsammlung / Curator of the Poster Collection
In Zusammenarbeit mit / In cooperation with
Petra Schmid, Publikationen / Publications
Museum für Gestaltung Zürich

© 2023
Zürcher Hochschule der Künste und Lars Müller Publishers

The museum of
Zurich University of the Arts
zhdk.ch

Museum für Gestaltung Zürich
Ausstellungsstrasse 60
Postfach
8031 Zürich, Switzerland
www.museum-gestaltung.ch

Museum für Gestaltung Zürich
Plakatsammlung / Poster Collection
sammlungen@museum-gestaltung.ch

Lars Müller Publishers
8005 Zürich, Switzerland
www.lars-mueller-publishers.com

ISBN 978-3-03778-730-4
Erste Auflage / First edition

Printed in the Netherlands

**Wir danken für Unterstützung /
For their support we thank:**

POSTER COLLECTION

 01 **REVUE 1926**

 02 **DONALD BRUN**

 03 **POSTERS FOR EXHIBITIONS 1980–2000**

 04 **HORS-SOL**

 05 **TYPOTECTURE**

 06 **VISUAL STRATEGIES AGAINST AIDS**

 07 **ARMIN HOFMANN**

 08 **BLACK AND WHITE**

 09 **RALPH SCHRAIVOGEL**

 10 **MICHAEL ENGELMANN**

 11 **HANDMADE**

 12 **CATHERINE ZASK**

 13 **TYPO CHINA**

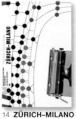 14 **ZÜRICH–MILANO**

 15 **BREAKING THE RULES**

 16 **COMIX!**

 17 **PHOTO GRAPHICS**

 18 **OTTO BAUMBERGER**

 19 **HEAD TO HEAD**

 20 **HELP!**

 21 **PARADISE SWITZERLAND**

 22 **LETTERS ONLY**

 23 **IN SERIES**

 24 **THE MAGIC OF THINGS**

 25 **JOSEF MÜLLER-BROCKMANN**

 26 **JAPAN – NIPPON**

 27 **THE HAND**

 28 **HERBERT LEUPIN**

 29 **HAMBURGER – STAEHELIN**

 30 **SELF-PROMOTION**

 31 **STOP MOTION**

 32 **EN VOGUE**

 33 **JA! NEIN! YES! NO! SWISS POSTERS FOR DEMOCRACY**

 34 **NIKLAUS TROXLER**